Inside The Mind Of Sexual Offenders

Inside The Mind Of Sexual Offenders:

Predatory Rapists, Pedophiles, And Criminal Profiles

Dennis J. Stevens, Ph.D.

Authors Choice Press

San Jose New York Lincoln Shanghai

Inside The Mind Of Sexual Offenders:
Predatory Rapists, Pedophiles, And Criminal Profiles

Authors Choice Press
an imprint of iUniverse.com, Inc.

For information address:
iUniverse.com, Inc.
5220 S 16th, Ste. 200
Lincoln, NE 68512
www.iuniverse.com

ISBN: 0-595-20046-X

Printed in the United States of America

Dedicated to all the wonderful little women in my life—
My daughter, Alyssa P. Stevens and my granddaughter, Danielle Stevens

EPIGRAPH

OTHER BOOKS BY
DENNIS J. STEVENS

Applied Community Policing in the 21st Century (Allyn Bacon, in Press)

Applied Community Corrections in the 21st Century (Prentice Hall, in Press)

Case Studies in Community Policing (Prentice Hall)

Policing and Community Partnerships [Editor] (Prentice Hall)

Corrections Perspective [Editor] (Coursewise)

Inside the Mind of the Serial Rapist (Austin & Winfield)

Contents

Part I 1

Chapter 1 Introduction 3

Believing Criminals 3

Sharing Some Thoughts 6

Uniqueness of this study 7

Chapter Order 8

Objectives 9

Definition of Serial Rape 10

The Victim 11

How Many Victims Are There? 12

Why Victims Don't Report Serial Rape 13

Chapter 2 Myths 17

General Myths About Serial Rape 17

Myth One The Fear of Rape 17

Myth Two Population Increases Causes More Serial Rape 21

Myth Three Legalize Prostitution 22

Myth Four Criminals Disrespect Law and Order 23

Myth Five Money, Cops, and Crime Control 24

Myth Six Violent Crime is Declining 25

Myth Seven Lock'em Up 27

Chapter 3 Causes 30

An Overview: The Causes of Serial Rape 30

Social Role Inequalities and Cultural Perspectives 30

Psychological Predisposition 31

Biological Perspectives 32

Social Learning 32

Subculture 33

Revenge and Sex 34

Summary 34

Chapter 4 Findings 36
Admitting Serial Rape 36
Motives of Serial Rapists 38
Lust 38
Righteous Rape 41
Peer Rape 45

Chapter 5 Control, Supremacy, and Fantasy 48
Control and Anger 48
Supremacy 49
Fantasy Rape 52
"Other" Rape 53
Summary 54

Chapter 6 Selection Techniques 56
Victim Selection 56
Easy Prey 57
Young Girls as Easy Prey 58
Middle Class Females as Easy Prey Victims 60
Occupational Tracking and Easy Prey 61
Shoppers as Easy Prey 62
Females Who Decrease Their Defense Capabilities 63
Random 63
Situational Targeting 66
Confusing Statements 69
Target Conclusions 70

Chapter 7 violence and serial rape 72
Overview of Violence 72
Descriptions of Violence 73

Unclear Violence Levels 75
Nonviolence 75
Intimidation 76
Limited Violence 76
Moderate Violence 78
Ultimate Violence 79
Conclusion 81

Chapter 8 Excessive Force 83
Introduction of Excessive Force 83
Assumptions 84
Excessive Force Offenders 84
conclusion 90
University Student Evaluation 95
Method and Sample 97
Student-Interviewers 97
Criminal Validity 98
Type of Questions 100
Who Were The Offenders In This Study? 102
Data Collection 104
Interviews 104
Limitations of This Study 105
Race of Victims 106

Chapter 9 Inside the Head of a Rapist 108

Chapter 10 Serial Rape Conclusion 115
References 120

Part II 127
Chapter 11 A Case Study of Three Generations of
             Predatory Sexual Offenders 129

Introduction 129
Psychopaths and Antisocial Personality Disorders 130
Incarceration of Sexual Offenders 132
Methodology 134
Findings 135
    Stephen King 136
    Andrea Evert 139
    Milton Evert 140
    Larry Evert 141
    Lindsey Truman 144
    Henry George Truman 145
    Collin Truman 146
    Tamara Evert 149
    Jason King 150
Discussion 151
References 155

Chapter 12 Predatory Pedophiles: A Case Study 161
Introduction 161
Statistics 163
Legislation 163
Control Strategies 164
Personality Tests 166
Sample 166
    Larry Evert 167
    Jason King 169
    Sully Lexington 169
Natural Sexuality 170
Problematic Sexuality 171
Explanations of Criminal Conduct 175
Realities of Pedophiles: Goals 180
What Has Been Learned 183

References 185

Chapter 13 Criminal Profiles 190
Introduction 190
The Sample 191
Predators 194
Findings 195
    Control Offenders 199
    Righteous Offenders 200
    Situational 203
    Revenge 204
    Visionary Offenders 206
Conclusion 207

FOREWORD

In *Inside the Mind of Sexual Offenders*, Dennis J. Stevens provides what maybe the most realistic and comprehensive approach to the study of rape and serial rapists available to readers today. Rape, says Stevens, is far too often understood only in highly politicized terms. The jargon and perspectives that have been developed over the past 30 years to understand the motivations of rapists, Stevens tells us, have too frequently been built upon idealized political and social posturing by special interest groups. Such arm-chair theorizing, while it may lend itself to politically correct explanations of rape, is commonly removed from the realm of offender motivation, and the reality of rape itself.

Stevens analyzes traditional beliefs about rape by asking questions such as "Is rape a tool of male power intended to keep women in subservient roles, or is it the carnal expression of lust subjectively experienced and acted upon by inadequately socialized individuals?

Most instructive is Stevens' use of participant self-reports; that is, information from rapists themselves–collected through interviews with more than 60 serial offenders. Interestingly, Stevens' methodology was to employ convicted felons as interviewers in order to avoid being "conned" by his subjects. Stevens sets the theme for the entire book in the preface when he writes, "My aim is to tell you what I have learned about this crime from the mouths of men who have committed it."

Stevens' debunking of rape "myths," especially those which lead to fear and passivity among victims, is worthwhile reading all by itself because it questions many contemporary assumptions about rape. According to Stevens, debunking such myths empowers women, making them more capable of successfully avoiding and resisting rape.

Especially worthwhile, however, is the qualitative interview information that Stevens has gathered. As a result of intimate interviews with actual rapists, *Inside the Mind of Sexual Offenders* offers a fresh, close-to-the-source, form of really understanding rape. Chapters such as "Inside the Head of a Rapist" are replete with insights into the thought processes of offender motivation developed by Stevens lead to new typologies of rapists, rapist motivations, and rape victims. Stevens' typologies offer insightful guidance for future research, and can surely help policy makers in planning programs to prevent rape as well as in the handling of convicted rapists.

Inside the Mind of Sexual Offenders provides a fresh perspective on the crime of forcible rape–and the motivation behind it. This book is a "must read" for anyone interested in better understanding this often misinterpreted crime. Thank goodness for writers like Dennis J. Stevens who is a colleague and a friend.

Frank Schmalleger, Ph.D.
Director
The Justice Research Association
Hilton Head, South Carolina

PREFACE

This book is about sexual offenders. Not the ones on television or at your local movie theater. These are real violators engaged in compulsive criminally violent behavior including abduction, serial rape, sexual homicide, necrophilia, and other grotesque acts visited upon a vulnerable American population whose justice system fails to control. That is, *Inside the Mind of a Sexual Offender* departs from an antiseptic world of fiction for a frightening glimpse through the eyes of men, women, children who like cross-eyed creatures lurking on a different plane of existence see their wickedness through a mask of sanity.

This work contains a full disclosure of three generations of incarcerated sexual offenders, from grandparents to their grandchildren, who committed the most horrendous acts towards others. In fact, there is no way of knowing how many victims this family assaulted, but in the final analysis there are specifics that you will come to understand about them that may change your point of view about that ultimate punishment available to us. The chapter on predatory pedophiles is a case study of three predators ranging in age from 17 to 52. It reveals the realities of pedophiles and explains why most pedophiles are rarely apprehended, and if they are, why they are eventually released from custody.

Finally, the last chapter is about criminal profiles of incarcerated offenders who have committed crimes of murder, rape, child molestation and other crimes of violence, and yet, our justice system, regrettably, has few clues about the extent of their criminal lifestyles.

The work in this book is about discussions you don't want to have with anyone, let alone a stranger! My aim is to tell you what I have learned about these horrible crimes from the mouths of men and women who committed them.

It all started one day when I dashed up the steps to my criminology class at the University of South Carolina on a sultry afternoon in early

May. I froze in stride when a huge sign leaped these words at me: ALL MEN ARE POTENTIAL RAPISTS, BEWARE!

As I addressed my students, I looked at the young men in that auditorium and knew instantly that there was a huge difference between them and the prisoners I left in "group" earlier in the day at one of the south's highest custody penitentiaries. "No," I cried silently at no one and everyone, and decided then and there to examine this matter. After reading every article I could get my hands on, I realized the power brokers turned the study of rape and pedophilia into a political obsession instead of a criminal investigation. Rape, they said, is a devise used by aggressive men to enslave women. "Keep women in their place," the volumes of literature said. I guessed some women were no longer willing to accept the lead of aggressive men. Maybe they shouldn't, but all men surely don't want to control women or children. Angry women, and some should be, apparently think differently! As evidenced by that sign at the top of those steps which led to the auditorium and my university students, angry women stirred some concerns inside me demanding inquiry.

Determined to investigate further serial rape and pedophilia, I recalled earlier advice given by my patient professors at Loyola University of Chicago who explained that when a researcher wants to inquire about something— go to the source. They argued that secondary sources could alter truth. I took that to mean that if I wanted to know if students were happy, don't ask parents or teachers, ask students. If I want to know about crime, for heavens sake, don't ask cops, they're not criminals, ask the experts-by-experience— criminals! I did. In fact, I also trained inmate-students to ask other criminally violent offenders about predatory rape and pedophilia. One conclusion I came away with from this investigation was that this book must be written without all the academic icons and political fluff.

September 26, 2001
Dennis J. Stevens, Ph.D.
Boston

ACKNOWLEDGEMENTS

Thomas B. Priest at Johnson C. Smith University provided inspiration to complete this work. Michael Shone at the University of South Carolina and Don C. Gibbons at Portland State College spent considerable time editing parts of the materials which eventually became chapters in this work. Sammy Catch from Mount Olive College helped with the fuzzy parts of my conclusion. My mother Joann Stevens and my sister Suzanne Koller delivered frequent encouragement. Lastly, every time I held my wonderful daughter Alyssa, I was driven to complete these pages.

Grateful acknowledgement is given to the following publications in which articles in this volume originally appeared in some form or another.

Violence and Serial Rape. *Journal of Police and Criminal Psychology*, 12(1), 39-47. 1997.

Motives of Serial Rape. *Free Inquiry in Creative Sociology*, 23(2), 117-126. 1995.

Explanations of Excessive Force Used During Serial Rape Attacks. *Criminologist*. 1998.

Predatory rape and victim targeting techniques. *The Social Science Journal*, 31 (4), 421-433. 1994.

Interviews with Women Convicted of Murder: Battered Women Syndrome Revisited. *International Review of Victiminology*, 6(2), 117-135. 1999.

Three Generations of Sexual Offenders. In Dennis J. Stevens (Ed.) *Corrections Perspective*, Madison, WI: Coursewise Publications.

Identifying Criminal Predators, Sentences, and Criminal Classifications. *Journal of Police and Criminal Psychology*, 15(1), 50-71.

Part I

CHAPTER 1

Introduction

Believing Criminals

Criminals lie! But there is something begging to be heard from them. The real question is iwhat's in it for them to lie about criminal activities especially if an inmate is telling his stories to another convicted felon? Would reckless stories about crime make other inmates admire or despise him? Let's see, if you're an resident of a maximum custody penitentiary with a lot of time on your hands and living daily with 1,500 of the worst lot of men, what would you tell them?

    A. Build your criminal ventures
    B. Keep a low profile
    C. Brag about beating grandmothers into sexual submission
    D. Reveal stories that could hurt parole opportunities
    E. Tell stories about sexual encounters with children

Selection 'B' is probably a prudent response. Would you exaggerate the circumstances of a crime you were never tried for, knowing prosecution could be near? The obvious truth is that it is harder to get a rapist to talk about his criminal activities particularly if he had never been charged with the crime. Prisoners have two jobs:

• Keep a clean record in order to be released
• Survival

Would making up stories to look good to other inmates get you back on the street faster?

In general, rapists are looked upon as "weak," said William Grace, one of two lifers who helped guide my work, and who protected my interests on several occasions. "First," said he, "if they were convicted for rape that means they didn't have control of their women. Second, they had to resort to short cuts to get sex. Only wimps need to attack for sex," he added. Thomas Crooks Jr., another inmate I am indebted too, advised, "in prisons like this, being macho means survival, and part of machismo is having ladies around when you were on the street that loved your ass." That's the other job inmates have in maximum custody confinement—survival. Convicted rapists are usually segregated from the other prisoners as they come under attack a lot of the time, especially men who raped children. Let me explain it another way.

When I worked at Stateville, a notorious maximum custody penitentiary near Chicago, the prisoners bet that the life of John Wayne Gacy would end in less than 52 seconds if he were in general prison population.

His living quarters were segregated from all other inmates, and he was guarded 24-7 by a special task force of correctional officers.[1] On the other hand, at the same penitentiary, Richard Speck, who had vigorously attacked, raped, and killed several nurses (including my next-door neighbor's cousin), in their Chicago apartment, painted the walls outside my

---

1. Gacy had buried the body parts of many young boys under his home in a suburb of Chicago. He was finally put to death (May, 1994) by the State of Illinois almost 13 years after being captured. But, an inmate at Columbia Correctional in Wisconsin got to Jeffrey Dahmer despite protective custody and killed him on November 28, 1994. That entire episode took less than 60 seconds.

prison classroom at Stateville and was safe in general prison population. Inmates have their own sense of justice.

While there are always exceptions to every rule, it appears the accounts of rape and child molestation by incarcerated inmates might be underestimates of their activities. I'm in good company concerning the underreporting of rape attacks by rapists as other researchers also find that rapists tend to say less about sexual offenses than other inmate offenders.[2]

However, being suspicious of criminals is always a good idea because they are, indeed, criminals! They lie, cheat, hurt, rob, rape, and murder people without a blink or a moment of thought. Yet, as you examine their narratives, remember there are limitations of their accounts as they relate only to apprehended criminals and serial sexual offenders and not to other types of criminals or to other types of rapists such as date rapists. Clearly, acceptance of fresh ways of getting at truth especially of rape-behavior seems to be obscured by both rape-politics and myths produced by fear entrepreneurs who sensationalize serial rape. But, by ignoring narratives offered by serial rapists, is it possible that knowledge could be lost? Or do we move forward and borrow a thought from a colleague who said:

> Rape is prevented by accurate knowledge about its causes, and accurate knowledge can only be obtained by the objective examination of evidence and the skeptical evaluation of conclusions based on that evidence.[3]

Yet, there seems to be something odd in the air when some researchers talk about past experiences and future expectations of serial rapists. Those

---

2. For a closer review of this perspective see Scully (1990) and MacKinnon (1987).

3. Crag Palmer (1988)

researchers seem to combine all forms of rape activity or examine it in clinical laboratories. Sometimes researchers make general statements suggesting that the motivation for predatory rape and date rape are similar. I would imagine that a predator hunting victims down like dogs has a different goal than a high school senior trying to impress his friends! I would also speculate that if we ask victims, cops, or dip into criminal files, each might have something important to share about how a predator picks prey. But, I also want to hear from individuals who have done the hunting before I feel that I've learned something about the hunt.

Sharing Some Thoughts

Let me share my personal thoughts with you, in confidence, about those attacks as described by chronic rapists and child molesters. When I heard about them the first time, my feelings changed. First, I felt pain. I also felt a helplessness that I could not protect their victims. Second, I prayed for the power to help those victims, but realized there was nothing I could do to change the experiences of those individuals. Third, I felt frustrated–frustrated that my sky-god permitted individuals to irrevocably alter the experiences of innocent people; and anger—anger that some of those self-centered predators felt pity and remorse for their victims, but they did it anyways. Fourth, I felt the horror of submission of their victims and wished there were something I could do to prevent victimization. Finally, and thank you for indulging me, after many sessions with those criminally violent offenders, I thought I was tough since I experienced much (as many of us have)–but, caught myself with both, tears in my hands and the steering wheel of my vehicle as I drove home from prison over the past 14 years.

Uniqueness of this study

Some psychologists, sociologists, and/or retired FBI agents examined the nuances of serial rape much like sliding a Buick through the eye of a needle. They developed a reasonable theory about serial rapists in their offices; collected and analyzed information at police stations and libraries; and linked those findings to support existing popular viewpoints about serial rapists. What makes my work unique is that I revised the process and let the theory arise from the information I gained in the penitentiary and: (1) exclusively examined serial rape and pedophilia; (2) rather than asking victims or reviewing records–predatory sexual offenders were consulted; (3) data were obtained through convicted felons trained as interviewers; (4) ideas about rape motivation, target selection, and violence emerged from the offenders; (5) university students,[4] cops, and criminologists helped evaluate the stories of the offenders, and (6) solutions to curb serial rape came from offenders rather then psychologists, sociologists, or FBI agents. Additionally, the entire study lasted many years and took place at many penitentiaries including CCI in Columbia, SC; Eastern and Central in NC; Attica and Gowanda in NY; Norfolk and Bay State in MA; Stateville and Joliet in Chicago; and women's prisons in Lauren, SC; Raleigh, NC, and Framingham, MA.

---

4. See Appendix 1 for more detail on this process

Chapter Order

This book is arranged in such a way as to guide you easily through the number of complex issues surrounding serial rape, pedophilia, three generations of sexual offenders, and finally a classification system of high risk offenders. There are two part to this work: Part I consists of Chapters 1 through 10 deals excessively with serial rape and issues arising from that subject. Specifically, Chapter 1 is an introduction to serial rape, it discusses the typical victim, the number of predatory rape attacks, and offers some incites as to why victims do not report predatory rape. Chapter 2 presents some general myths about predatory rape and how mythical official policy might curb it; for instance, there is a discussion on articles in popular women magazines that encourages victim submission while promoting and reinforcing a learned helplessness among women. Chapter 3 considers a number of rival theories that try to explain predatory rape but miss reality. Chapter 4 presents an explanation of serial rape through the use of six serial rape categories. This chapter offers explanations about three of those categories including lust, righteous, and peer rape. Chapter 5 offers a discussion of control/anger, supremacy, and fantasy rape. Chapter 6 discusses victim selection techniques used by predators and how to avoid rape. Chapter 7 clarifies a serial rapist's use of physical force and Chapter 8 explains in detail why some offenders use excessive force, commit necrophilla, and cannibalism. This chapter includes a discussion on why predators embrace evil during some of the ruthless attacks and the presents the issues suggesting that sexual offenders may well have a sexual addiction. Chapter 9 offers a narrative about the daily life of a rapist. Chapter 10 offers a conclusion and recommendations based on the findings of this work relative to serial rapists including the use of drugs to chemically castrate sexual offenders as one method of dealing with sexual addiction.

Appendix 1 shows how university students helped this project by evaluating the accounts of the rapists. Appendix 2 discusses the research design or method I used and information about obtaining the sample in this study, student-interviewers, and criminal validity concerns. Appendix 3 shows the types of questions used during the interview process, and Appendix 4 describes the characteristics of the offenders in the sample and includes a table for your convenience.

Part II consists of Chapters 11 through Chapter 13. Specifically, Chapter 11 offers a study about three generations of sexual offenders and their accounts spanning an enormous number of years and compulsive behaviors ending in the victimization of an uncountable number of men, women, and children. Chapter 12 presents a narrative about pedophilia complete with examples, explanations, and a conclusion. Chapter 13 presents a classification of sexual offenders that can aid you in better understanding their conduct.

Objectives

When a reader finishes this book, he or she will be able to relate to the major interpretations of serial rape offered by the popular writers in the field and will have a comprehensive view about serial rape from the perspective of the offenders. A reader will see evidence suggesting that "fear entrepreneurs" promote and reinforce both the fear of rape and a learned helplessness among females that aid predators during their attacks. A reader will see the evidence suggesting that politically correct theory has little to do with criminal reality and less to do with crime control. It will become clear that serial rape is not a single isolated event in the life of a rapist, but that it is an ongoing series of conscious lifestyle decisions made by him. A reader will see how some rapists embrace evil suggesting that America is moving into an unhealthy and unholy society since public violence has become private violence and is heading toward collective violence. A reader will realize that a velvet glove and dagger approach is necessary to control predators–effective prevention and persuasive punishment.

Some readers will learn how to avoid becoming a serial rape target, and some will gain an insight into another one of our growing problems—a psychological dependence or addiction of sexual encounters. At the conclusion of this book, a reader will understand why the following recommendations are being offered: classifying sexual offenders as addicts, controlling sexual offenders through chemical castration with drugs such as depo-provera, educating females about learned helplessness, identifying all sexual offenders in the community, eliminating plea-bargaining, mandatory life sentences in segregation, and frequent use of capital punishment.

Definition of Serial Rape

One official definition of rape is carnal knowledge through the use of force or the threat of force. When it happens more than once by the same offender, I call it serial rape. But sometimes predators fail in their attempts to rape a stranger for many reasons. They attack many females, some they know and some they don't. Serial rapists coerce others into submission through intimidation and manipulation. That is sometimes they lie, misrepresent, or to put it plainly-smooth talk victims into sexual encounters. In fact, a victim might think she is doing something of her own free-will when in reality she had been led to believe a lie; other times, a female thinks she can control a male and discovers, much to their regret, she was easy pray. Therefore, informed consent should be part of every rape definition. And, the priorities of some rapists, due to premature ejaculation or individual rationalizations prohibit many of them from performing sexual intercourse. All forms of sexual contact should be included in a definition of serial rape. The terms stranger, serial, predatory, and forcible rape will be interchangeable descriptions of serial rape. Therefore, for the purposes of this work, predatory or serial rape will refer to the coerced attempt or actual sexual contact of others without their informed consent.

The Victim

The serial rapist can attack any aged female or male for that matter, regardless of his or her physical condition or the company she or he is in (for the balance of the discussion, since females are attached more often, this work will refer to females as victims). Predatory rapists attack females who are unconscious, recovering from surgery, young, old, attractive, or women whose physical attributes are unknown to them. They attack females in the commission of other felons such as break-ins and armed robberies. They attack white females more often black females. That is, in 1995, approximately 240,820 white victims reported being rape victims as compared with 61,290 black victims, says the Bureau of Justice Statistics.[5] However, it could be that while white women reported forcible rape more often than black women did since black women in general have a lower opinion of law enforcement than do white women.

Predatory rapists attack females who are alone, females who are with friends, women with their husbands and children with their parents at restaurants. They attack females when they work, walk, and even when they help others. They attack females who are in public places such as shopping malls. Private places such as restrooms and safe places such as recovery rooms at hospitals. But mostly, they attack females whom they perceive as vulnerable or females whom they intimidate into what they consider a vulnerable situation.

---

5. Bureau of Justice Statistics (BJS), (1997) shows that of the white victims, 122,700 rapes were completed and 118,120 failed (49%) as compared to 35,510 were completed and 25,380 failed (41%) among black victims.

How Many Victims Are There?

It's difficult to tell how many females or men or children have been raped since forcible rape statistics are confusing and most victims never report their attack. There are many statistical equations available, and it's a matter of which one you want to believe. There are two reliable contributors to rape statistics: police reports and victimization reports.

Police records are established from victim reports to local police agencies. Those agencies relate the information to the U.S. Department of Justice, but they are not under an obligation to do so nor are their reports necessarily accurate. They produce finalized reports, which are distributed through the Bureau of Justice Statistics (BJS), and criminal victimization rates are measures of the occurrence of victimization among a specified population group. Those results are also reported to the U.S. Department of Justice and published by BJS[6] and the FBI's Uniform Crime Reports. Both set of statistics can be found on-line at http://www.ojp.usdoj.gov/bjs/

BJS breaks down rape reports by stranger rape and nonstranger rape. For instance, they estimated that almost 175,000 rapes were reported to the police in 1995. Of those reports, approximately 52% (90,300) were stranger rapes. BJS showed that 30,480 were completed stranger rapes and 59,820 were attempted stranger rapes. They estimated that there were more rape attacks by strangers than nonstrangers, but strangers failed at

---

6. BJS (1997). This reference is available online: http://www.albany.edu/sourcebook/ or victimization reports available online: http://www.albany.edu/source-book/1995/ind/VICTIMIZATION.Rape.Number.2.html or from the US Department of Justice by calling 1(800)732-3277 and asking for NCJ1258900 (a $6.00 charge will apply).

their attempts more often than did nonstrangers.[7] Also, chronic rapists attack females they knew such as their wives and their children.

Victimization reports show that almost 40% or another 70,000 victims never reported rape attacks to anyone including to the police. Other estimators suggest that 60% of rape victims never report it. One reason for the difference in the two calculations could partly relate to difference in the understanding of what constitutes rape. For example until 1993, South Carolina had not considered spouse rape an illegal act and many states have yet to pass such a law, and many who have, rarely enforce it. Perhaps, some women interpreted that the law reflected a level of morality and women raped by strangers in, what I call, spouse-rape-free states felt it unbefitting to report stranger rape since they couldn't report their spouse: why report a stranger?

Why Victims Don't Report Serial Rape

There are many reasons women don't report predatory rape. BJS guesses that 25% of the females who didn't report rape might say that their rape was a personal matter while another 10% would say that they thought they lacked proof. Eleven percent of the nonreporters of rape might reveal that they were afraid of reprisals from their attacker. Also, 2% of those unreported victims hadn't reported it because those victims felt the rape was an unimportant event. Other reasons might include shame and embarrassment, which the U.S. Department of Justice does not address.

The Department of Justice does not use the term serial rapists or predatory rapists for stranger rapists. That is, they do not break down the number of times a predator has attacked females, because they may never know. They know the police report initiated by the victim or witnesses. Many of the stranger rapes are indeed committed by serial rapists--individuals sexually attacking many females.

It might be safe to say that women fail to report being victimized due in part to their feelings that they would, again, be victimized by others. That is, once a woman is raped and tells: a spouse or an intimate-other, friends, parents, and/or the criminal justice community, she is treated differently. Her behavior can be translated into more guilt. For instance, it is common practice for law enforcement, social workers, hospital personnel, and defense lawyers to question her lifestyle prior to the sexual assault. Specifically, many individuals in decision-making roles think that her lifestyle before the attack had something to do with the crime. So, I guess that means if a prizefighter is attacked on the street, then it's not a crime!

Experience tells me that many victims fail to report all kinds of crimes including sexual assault in part due to feelings of self-blame. Victim self-blame or guilt may center on the way a victim dressed, smiled, or walked to her car after shopping at K-Mart. Some victims might think that had she changed something about herself, she would have never been a target. There's more!

Since women have been treated as inferior to males throughout most of their lives by their fathers, brothers, husbands, ministers, and other women (to name a few), she might consider her victimization as further proof of her inability to compete and to win against males.[8] Clearly, rape

8. Images of their inferiority are communicated in many different forms and in an enormous range of contexts beginning at an early age. These images are found in children's movies like the *Lion King* depicting females in exclusively helper roles, television shows like NYPD Blue depicting female detectives as drunks and incompetent, experiences at school and at the work place where men play most of the major roles as administrators and leaders. See Stevens (1998a) for more detail. Also, women convicted of homicide report losing their assets such as home, savings accounts, and personal items including their children to in-laws or the courts leaving a serious gap in their experiences and their financial opportunities to defend themselves. Also, when a female is arrested for the murder of her spouse, his family takes all of her assets making it impossible to win visitation rights let alone her murder defense. Oddly, there appears to be a Kafkaesque inquiry into who feels the pains of imprisonment more severe: females or males. See Stevens (1998b) for more detail.

does not prove that a female is inferior or at fault. Nonetheless, many victims think that by not reporting crimes against themselves that they won't be considered losers.

Lastly, some females especially young girls lack experience in telling parents about strangers which of course has a ring of truth to it the other way around, too. That is, experience in many abused children's centers tells us that some girls can't tell strangers about the horrible things their parents and/or guardians have done to them.

What all of the above means is that we may never know how many females or for that fact, how many males have been sexually attacked by strangers. But, a good guess is that the number of rape attacks is far greater than anyone expects or wants to entertain. I am always surprised how often in the classroom the number of females who come forward and explain how they were victimized but hadn't reported it because they felt they had brought the rape upon themselves or because they were afraid others would treat them differently. Statistics can't change the events some individuals have experienced nor can some victims be left to themselves. Evidently many victims have little desire in coming forward and perhaps, even when the justice community has good intentions,—those victims shouldn't! For instance, research has shown that mandatory arrest of domestic violence offenders leads to more, not less violence against victims.[9]

---

9. That is, spouse abusers who were arrested intensified their victimization after an arrest. Some of the methods they used included: night attacks, possessions of the victims such as cars, telephones, and clothes were destroyed; victims were isolated from friends, parents, and bank/credit accounts; and victims met with sexual assault from foreign objects, friends, and in some cases the children of the abusers. Most of the officers who interacted with victims and offenders were reluctant to intervene; they were apprehensive to make an arrest despite evidence suggesting they should; surprisingly enough, their behavior during the intervention appeared hostile to victims. Also, arrest had not protected victims from abuse and when victims fled from their homes, many of them sought out other abusers. see Stevens (1998d).

This chapter offers an insight into the many problems surrounding the definition of rape and explains the differences in police reports and victimization reports. How many rape victims there are is highly debatable. Clearly, the public has limited information to gage rape attacks. One reason it is difficult to tell the number of rapes due in part to the apprehensiveness of victims and their level of confidence they have for the criminal justice system. However, all estimates suggest that potential forcible rape attacks influence the way many women live. Thus, it is highly likely that many women habituate to avoid being a rape victim—again! Other factors why women don't report rape could relate to a sectional regard for law enforcement or cultural expectations. For example, some victims may feel that law enforcement is less likely to respond to rape reports in poverty section of a community and therefore those women might report it less often. Some writers estimate that 1 in 5 females might be sexually attacked sometime in her life and over one-half of those victims would be attacked by men they had never met.

As you can imagine, it is difficult to determine the actual number of rape attacks due to the number of unreported cases; I suppose this means that there are probably many more cases of rape unreported than expected.

CHAPTER 2

Myths

General Myths About Serial Rape

There are many legends or myths about serial rape and how to control it. This chapter examines some of the most common myths about predatory rape held by some readers. My intention is to address some of those myths and to answer some of your anticipated questions about this often misunderstood crime. For example, experiences in the university classroom are suggestive of something I refer to as the fear of rape. By that I mean that many students have admitted that they have been taught from a very young age that if attacked–submit; otherwise, attackers would hurt them. Many of the rapists I interviewed for this study liked that idea and implied that I do nothing to destroy that myth. "Who spread that rumor, Richard Speck or the Boston Strangler?" William Grace asked. My Gosh! Let's see, if a guy told me that he was about to shoot me, and he wanted me to stand still so he could get a better aim, I'd do it, right?

Myth One
The Fear of Rape

Some writers believe that women should fear their attackers and comply with their demands.[10] They believe that predatory rape is largely rooted in male power trips, personality flaws, and/or uncontrollable urges for violence. Those advocates argue that a strong relationship exists between sexual assault, offender violence, and victim surrender. The mission of a rapist can include the complete physical degradation of a victim. Therefore, they imply that a female should submit when sexually attacked because her attacker is a person who enjoys violence more than sex.

Consistent with this view are 141 articles about serial rape in the mainstream press from 1982 to 1995 which were reviewed for this study. Those publications include:

Ebony, Essence, Glamour, Good Housekeeping, Ladies Home Journal, Maclean's, Mademoiselle, McCalls, MS, Nations Business, Newsweek, NY Times Magazine, People Weekly, Psychology Today, Redbook, Reader's Digest, Scholastic Update, Time, and Teen.

Most of the titles on serial rape, linked wanton violence and rape together: for example, "Three Fearful Hours" in People Weekly, "The War on Women" in Scholastic Update, "A Betrayal of Trust" in Good Housekeeping, "Violence Against Women" in MS, and "I Just Want to Live in Reader's Digest. Other articles like "Why Do Men Rape" in Glamour, "Why Men Rape" in Mademoiselle, and "What's Behind the Dramatic Rise in Rapes" in Ebony report that power, anger, and torture are characterized in every rape and that violence is the main objective of the rapist, not sex. Other examples include "Inside the Mind of a Rapist" when an interviewed rapist implied that most of his victims did not fight back, the writer, Jeanie Kasindorf relied upon the interpretation of a

10. See Brownmiller, 1975; Burgess & Holmstrom, 1974; Ellis 1980; Groth, 1979; Storaska, 1975.

Brandeis psychologist who tied rape with sadism and anger. Part of her interpretation includes the perceptive that women should never fight back when attacked by a serial rapist because rapists are sadists who want to destroy women. In Psychology Today there are two articles, "Assertiveness Breeds Attempt" and "Eve's Punishment" which imply that women should play the role of a passive victim when attacked. Other articles depict heinous violence like "Fraternities of Fear: Gang Rape, Male Bonding, and the Silencing of Women" and "Femicide: Speaking the Unspeakable" in MS. These fear entrepreneurs, present similar messages as Caputi and Russell suggest in MS magazine:

> Rape is a direct expression of sexual politics, an assertion of masculinist norms, and a form of terrorism that preserves the gender status quo....Murder is simply the most extreme form of sexist terrorism.

Only 8 (6%) of 141 articles described resistance, and each of those articles emphasized delayed reaction. Of those articles discussing weapons, they said that the only women who carry them should be gun experts. Women will lose, those headlines shout! The compelling evidence offered above promotes and reinforces both the fear of rape and a learned helplessness among many females. That is, females learn that they are helpless against the initial uncontrollable assault of rape and no matter what they do—they lose.[11]

Some academics were featured in many publications especially Dr. Judith Siegel in Mademoiselle, Dr. Hobson director of the sex offender

---

11. For more information see Seligman (1975). Then, too, the attributional model of learned helplessness (Abramson, Seligman, & Teasdale, 1978) might be more applicable to rape victims. Learned helplessness begins with the perception that we can't control something important. The more we explain this lack of control in terms of internal, stable, and global attributions, the more likely we are to feel helpless and depressed.

programs at Connecticut Correctional Institute at Somers in Ebony, and Dr. Lizotte in Glamour. These writers insisted that fighting sexual attackers serves to antagonize the attacker and he will respond with more violence.

Newspapers, too, add to the fear of rape perspective by sensationalizing rape and violence.[12] For instance, several major city newspapers purposely report rape in generalized terms intensifying reader fears as most identify with the victims. Many readers see themselves as the victim when reading generalized reports. But, a newspaper reporter I know says that newspapers generalize to keep confidential the identity of the victim. Maybe so, but how often do victims remain unknown especially in celebrated cases like the victims of Mike Tyson, the Kennedy clan, and the Central Park attack in New York. Nonetheless, the press adds to the fear of rape perspective with their sensationalization of rape and reinforces victim learned helplessness. The problem is that television and radio newscasters tend to use newspapers and magazines as exclusive sources for information they relay to the public. The public generally receives exaggerated accounts of the rapists. Therefore, these writers conclude that women who fight an attacker could be killing themselves. If you get the sense after reading this exercise that some mainstream publications are in business to make money by frightening women, I'd agree with you.

In summary, according to my way of thinking, the fingers keying stories unto computer screens for many newspaper and magazine articles are the same fingers helping predators terrorize victims. If these fear entrepreneurs are right, then most of serial rapists should be violent men whose goal is nothing more than beating women senseless and any sexual behavior is instrumental to their violence.

---

12. See Gordon & Riger (1989).

Myth Two
Population Increases Causes More Serial Rape

Some population advocates believe that as the American population grows, so does the rate of serial rape. With more people—it looks like more crime, they argue. If they're right, population and predatory rape increases should be somewhat parallel in their escalation rates.

The American population in 1971 was 206,212,000. In 1991, it was 252,177,000. That's a gain of 45,965,000 or 22%. Therefore, if the population increases impact rape, then serial rape should show similar percentile increases over a twenty year period.

In 1971, the U.S. Department of Justice reported 42,260 forcible rapes. In 1991, they reported 106,590 rapes. That is, 64,330 more rapes, twenty years later. A few calculations say that this increase represents approximately an increase of 152% rapes. Would victims report more rape in 1991 than in 1971? Chances are, they reported more in 1971 than in 1991 despite victimization reports showing that in 1971 approximately 49% of the rape victims reported as compared to 1991 when 59% reported. For instance, when examining surveys taken by the National Opinion Research Center in both 1973 (1971 isn't available) and 1991, fewer women in 1991 as opposed to 1973 had confidence in the police doing their jobs, say government statistics. That is, since more women were confident about police activities in 1971, it is reasonable that more of them reported rape then as opposed to a time when they had less certainty in the police.

Nonetheless, somehow, 22% versus 152% says something about the idea that population and rape are related variables. Yes, there are statisticians who can make these calculations say something else, but perhaps they calculate the same way the "fear of rape" peddlers do! In sum, significant correlation is virtually nonexistent between the increases in the American population and the increases in forcible rape levels especially when in various cities where populations have decreased over a twenty year period like Chicago and Detroit, yet rape rates have made steadily gains, says government statistics.

Myth Three
Legalize Prostitution

If prostitution were legal, forcible rape would be reduced. In a sense, these advocates imply that if prostitution were legal then they expect to see less forcible rape per capita (per 100,000 inhabitants) in areas where prostitution is legal as compared to areas where it is not legal. Reviewing forcible rape figures for Las Vegas, Nevada, a city serviced by legalized prostitution, there were 433 rapes in 1991. Las Vegas is a city like no other city in the United States as it attracts millions of tourists year around. However, cities like Miami, Honolulu, and New Orleans have many similarities to Las Vegas including a pleasant climate. But, Miami's rape rate was 253, Honolulu had 275, and New Orleans had 302 rapes in 1992. In relationship to their respective state populations since state populations may render a broader picture of state activities, the forcible rape rate per 100,000 inhabitants is as follows: 66.0 Nevada, 51.7 Florida, 33.0 Hawaii, 40.9 Louisiana. It is clear that rape is a crime out of control in Nevada, and Nevada permits prostitution.

On the other side of the prostitute's coin, all four cities in reality have prostitutes. Therefore, it is a trite question if prostitution were legal or not. However, in Las Vegas, like Miami, Honolulu, and New Orleans, the degradation of women through advertisements is constant, yet it's clearly part of what makes Las Vegas what it is; accordingly, its forcible rape rate is higher than Miami, Honolulu, and New Orleans, cities where tourists are as common as prostitutes.

I think it safe to suggest that legalizing prostitution would not deter serial rapists and might increase first time offenders by marketing women's bodies the way Burger King markets burgers. It should be noted that the general crime index in Miami, Honolulu, and New Orleans was greater than Las Vegas, but forcible rape was the crime of choice in Las Vegas probably due to the exploitation of all women.

Myth Four
Criminals Disrespect Law and Order

Criminal justice advocates might assert that criminals do not respect law and order and, therefore, commit crimes. However, public opinion polls such as one conducted by the General Social Surveys in 1972 where 27,782 interviews were conducted by the National Opinion Research Center, explain that when people were asked: How much respect do you have for the police in your area? Their responses show that 77% said a great deal, 17% said some, 04% selected very little as their answer and 02% claimed they don't know.

In 1992, when people were asked the same question by the same organization, 60% said a great deal, 32% said some, 7% responded with a hardly and 1% weren't sure how much they respected law enforcement. Obviously, public opinion, in general, about police is low. Also, when the public were asked: How would you rate the police in your community of the following…being helpful and friendly? Only 29% of the subjects said excellent, 45% said pretty good, 19% said only fair, 6% poor, and the balance weren't sure or refused to respond. Additionally, when asked, about police and crime prevention, 16% said excellent, 42% pretty good, 28% only fair, 13% poor, and 1% weren't sure. Therefore, we might say that these myth peddlers are partly right. Criminals might have low opinions of law enforcement, but so does everyone else. Therefore, it is safe to assume that Americans see little relationship between law enforcement and crime control.

Myth Five
Money, Cops, and Crime Control

Law enforcement supporters claim that more cops would mean fewer criminals. These folks say that if they can get huge increases in public funding, they could hire more officers and make a stand for truth, justice, the American way! Is there a relationship between number of cops, operating costs, and crime? If law enforcement advocates are right, then forcible rape counts and Total Crime Index rates would decrease as more money is spent. Each year, aside from a typical cost of living increase, as more money is spent to control crime, rape, and other criminally intense crimes should be effected.

Let's make this simple. In 1970, there were 534,537 state employees working in law enforcement with an operating cost of $6,026,948,000. In 1990, the U.S. Department of Justice reveals that there were 793,020 state employees working in law enforcement in 16,961 police agencies of all types at an operating cost of $41,550,270,000 across the United States. That is, 258,483 or an increase of 48% more people working in law enforcement with an increase cost of $35,523,332 or 589% increases.

Violent Crime Index? 363.5 per 100,000 inhabitants in 1970 to 758.1 per 100,000 inhabitants in 1991 or an increase of 394.6 per 100,000 inhabitants. Therefore, in 20 years, crime per capita had increased by 108%. In the same period of time, forcible rape went from 7.9 to 42.3 per 100,000 inhabitants or an increase of 435%. Added to this burden of more crime was the burden of 258,000 more persons earning a pay check in law enforcement which amounted to a cost increase of 589% in expenses.

Can law enforcement under its current operating procedures control crime, especially violent crime? Turning this question inside out, the real question is: how afraid are serial rapists of being apprehended by the police?[13] What we are likely to see is that serial rapists are more afraid of women who fight when attacked more than of being arrested. There were almost more uncompleted attempts of rape due to self protection measures employed by victims of rape (35,280 without the aid of a gun or a badge) than there were rape arrests in 1991 (40,120 arrests for all types of rape at a cost that stagers the imagination). Nether money nor number of law enforcement officers are related to Total Crime Index or the number of forcible rapes.

Myth Six
Violent Crime is Declining

Myth Five claims that violent crime is declining in the United States. I've encountered this perspective often and while writing this book one newspaper I read often had an article proclaiming that violent crime was really going down as opposed to up. To bring evidence to that point, the headline of this major newspaper read, "Who Says Crime Is Up?" The article detailed how the National Crime Victimization Survey is the best measure of crime trends. The message its numbers tell, the reporter wrote, was heartening and contrary to conventional crime wave wisdom. Specially, the reporter showed that all crimes had declined by 6% since 1973. Household crime crimes were down by 3% and personal theft by 18%. He pointed out that actual number of victimizations had increased

---

13. High-risk offenders who have been apprehended for crimes of violence say that the threat of prison is not a deterrence of crime. Some criminals use the system as a way to enhance their own reputations. See Stevens (1992a). Also, high-risk offenders who had committed and were apprehended for heinous crimes of violence believe in capital punishment. Fact is, most career criminals have their own hard line notions of justice, which do not include a court of appeal, plea bargaining, or reprieves. See Stevens (1992b)

by 24% over the past 20 years. The article reflected the wisdom of Dr. George Cole, a political scientist at the University of Connecticut, who claimed that only 39% of all crime in 1992 had been reported to police. Therefore, the 2.5 million violent crimes reported to the police were really 61% greater as indicated by victimization reports. However, Cole argues that according to the National Crime Victimization Survey, a collection of 166,000 interviews showed that the rate of crimes was consistently in decline over the last decade.

Could be! There are many experts who can help us through many uncertainties; some of those include prominent police advocates who proclaim that a police state will control crime and a Readers Digest senior editor, Eugene Methvin agrees with them. As for me, the first thing I tell my students is to scrutinize statistical sources. When something seems right, it's probably wrong. For example, the Total Crime Index shows that at a rate of 100,000 inhabitants in 1991 there were 5,897.8 crimes known to police. Sliding my finger through the various years to 1980, it showed 5,950.0 which of course represents more crime. Therefore, I could argue one point of view or if I desired to argue something different, I could present the figures from 1987 showing less crime per capita or 5,540.0 per 100,000 inhabitants. Should those figures not say what I want to say, I could offer Criminal Victimizations statistics or per capita calculations. Then, too, by using 1981 victimization reports, a peak crime year, we'll see a decline, for many crimes, but should we reference another year and compare that year to 1991 or 1992 we'll show a decline. Confused?

Also, should we compare victimization reports with police reports for specific years for specific crimes, we might make different conclusions about crime. That is, in 1973 49% of the rape victims reported the crime to police as compared with 41% in 1980, many more in 1981 (maybe that's why it was a peak crime year), and 59% reported rape in 1991. Also, in 1965 12.3 rapes were reported to the police per 100,000 of American inhabitants. In 1975, they rose to 26.3, in 1985 to 37.1, and in 1991 to 42.3 per 100,000 of our population. Additionally, there were almost

2,000,000 violent crimes committed suggesting that 758 individuals for every 100,000 people were victimized.

However, here's a shade of sad truth. In the peak crime year of 1981, 6.6 million violent victimizations were reported while in 1991, 6.4 million were reported. Saying all crime is down because specific crimes are down is misleading. In every major city across the United States, murder and forcible rape rates are jumping higher than each proceeding year over the past 20 years. How you argue crime or how you manipulate crime statistics, or how careless an argument might sound in the grasp of a statistical computation, the horrid fact remains that at no time in American history, are females more likely to become forcible rape victims than at any other time in U.S. history! Don't convince me with letters and reports suggesting my concerns are unfounded. One rape is too many if its your daughter or your mother, isn't it!

Myth Seven
Lock'em Up

The threat of prison will deter criminals from committing predatory rape is argued by many supporters who believe that incarceration reduces criminally violent activities. If the threat of prison worked, every time a felon was incarcerated, crime should be affected. In 1971, BJS reports that there were 177,113 men and women incarcerated in state prisons across the United States at an annual cost of $2,289,058,000. There were another 160,863 individuals in municipal and county jails. There were also 57,239 juveniles in detention facilities that year. All together, there were 395,215 men, women, and children in state custody.[14]

---

14. There were another 12,369 inmates in federal custody, but those statistics are unrelated to this discussion.

In 1991, 20 years later, there were 711,643 inmates, plus another 424,000 men and women in jail. Additionally, there were 66,132 juveniles in public and private detention facilities. The above totals suggest that there were 1,201,775 men, women, and children in custody. The total cost for state and local institutional confinement was $19,954,487,000 excluding probation and parole expenses. A few calculations say that confinement has increased by 806,560 individuals or an increase of 204% while expenses have increased by $17,665,429,000 or 771%. For the record there were also 64,000 inmates in federal prisons. By the by, in June 30, 1993 BJS shows another huge increase in the prison population totaling 925,247 inmates in both state and federal penitentiaries.

Violent crime has been affected—it went up. In 1971, violence jumped from 396.0 per 100,000 inhabitants to 758.1 for an increase of 362.1 per 100,000 inhabitants or 91%. In particular, forcible rape kicked up from 8.6 per 100,000 to 42.3 or 391%. But the central point is that confinement does not deter violent crime. When we consider it costs more to confine a criminal (which might not control crime) than to educate a child, something dreadfully is wrong.

Another point requiring attention about prison sentences is that when convicted criminals like career rapists are sent to prison, they continue to commit crime; but it's not reported and when it is, it's ignored by officials.[15] Therefore, crime is supposedly reduced on the streets, per say, but the habitual offenders have simply changed locations from one location where crime is more likely to be reported to another location where reporting is less likely. Serial rapists have changed their address, not their

---

15. For a closer look see Eichental & Jacobs (1991).

activities. And when these heinous criminals are released, their raping sprees of innocent individuals continues.

The behavior of criminals places them outside of community's care, and it's the criminal justice system that has direction of their welfare. But are we, the general population, victims again by the very system designed to protect us? Like law enforcement, corrections, too, has tricked us into believing that the criminal justice system works for the good of law abiding people and its clients, the criminals.

Yet, time and again, researchers find that the threat of prison time does not deter crime, especially violent crimes like serial rape. For example, in my own research at some of the toughest prisons in the United States-Attica in New York State and Stateville near Chicago, I learned that the criminal justice system perpetuates criminal activity by fueling anger through an ineffective, exploitative system of incarceration. The point is that many others know that too, so why isn't something done about it? Students often ask: "Since these things are known, then how come policy doesn't change?" I respond with, "Maybe those who set policy have other priorities? If you were in a position of power, what priorities would get in your way to do what's right?"

CHAPTER 3

Causes

An Overview: The Causes of Serial Rape

Official guidelines say that predatory rape largely includes descriptions about vaginal and anal penetration, cunnilingus, ejaculation, and fellatio; therefore, sexual offenders exhibiting those actions are classified as sexually dangerous. Nonetheless, a great deal of controversy continues about why men sexually assault strangers. My intention is to highlight a few of the major perspectives that may be representative of the vast literature about the causes of serial rape. Also, I've addressed some of the limitations of those views for your convenience. My brief list and their limitations are incomplete, as there are many variations relative to the causes of serial rape. But, I hope my brief outline will offer insight into the contradictorily study of serial rape.

Social Role Inequalities and Cultural Perspectives

Since antiquity, motivation leading to rape involves males wanting to keep women in their place, argue popular writers. The "real" motive of rape, these advocates say, is to preserve sexual role inequality through violence. Males, for example, use violence to rape in order to keep women in their subordinate role as barefoot and pregnant. Consistent with this view, is the thought that rape is used to keep women from gaining independence and autonomy, i.e., rape demonstrates that women are really the property of men. The predatory rapist is seen as part of a perspective whose focus is on interpersonal violence, male dominance, and sexual separation. In addition, sexual violence is an indicator of contempt that men have for female qualities. Rape is part of a culture of male violence.[16]

Psychological Predisposition

Related to male domination and control motivators, some psychologists argue that psychological and emotional factors predispose a person to react to situational and life events with sexual violence. They argue that there are three major patterns of behavior represented by rapists: power rape, anger rape, and sadistic rape, one being dominant in every instance. They conclude that there are few rapes where sex is the chief motivator. That is, sex is largely instrumental to the service of non-sexual needs. Using this psychological model of motivation, a rapist is a person who has serious psychological difficulties that hinder his relationship with others. In sadistic rape too, where the offender relishes physical harm to the victim, control is the primary motivating force for the offender. This model proposes that a rapist discharges his feelings of rejection and anger through sexual acting-out. This particular view was one that my students seemed anxious to hear about in the classroom as it confirms what the popular press says about the fear of rape perspectives offered earlier. In

---

16. See Brownmiller (1975) and Sanday (1981). Yet, refuting this view is data from preindustrial societies that show the existence of rape-free cultures. There might be some truth here, but I wonder if it were socially appropriate for women in those societies to report serial rape or not, and what would have happened if they had? For more information see Schwendinger and Schwendinger (1983) who offer a radical view. They say that in a capitalist society, their explanation about rape includes a form of exploitation of the politically weaker sex since men have and want to retain dominance. Since law determines rape's parameters, and men control the law, men control the sexuality of women.

fact, when I ask university students about the causes of predatory rape, they respond with ideas about control and power.[17]

Biological Perspectives

The attitudes of rapists toward women may not be particularly unusual, another group of exerts suggest. They say that rapists display specific attitudes and behavioral patterns of sexual arousal as compared to non-sexual offenders. This view says that coercion by violence is itself sexually arousing. Therefore, the motivation for rape apparently has to do with personality flaws inherited at birth. That is, many males cross a theoretical point called the forced copulation threshold due to neurological activities that are intimately linked with the effects of sex hormones upon brain functioning. Specifically, DNA molecules substantially influence the basic blue print of serial rapists. Also, a major part of this argument includes the notion that lower status males move beyond the forced copulation threshold more than other males.[18]

Social Learning

Operant conditioning or social learning views rape as resulting from the joint influences of cultural and experiential factors mediated by attitudes, sex role scripts, and other thought processes that link physical aggression and sexuality in the minds of males. In this view, aggression is instrumental or a devise rather than the goal itself, reports Albert Bandura

---

17. A. Nicholas Groth (1979) offers the best discussion on this view.

18. Of particular interest is both, Lee Ellis (1989) and Hans Eysenck and Gisli Gudjonsson's (1989) view concerning this argument.

(1973). Therefore, some rapists, Bandura's supporters would say, can have a genuine appetite for sex, but are socially trained to use violence to show that they are serious about their goals. However, the actual technique in committing rape is learned through a social learning process.[19]

On the other hand, social learning perspectives have a tendency to be deterministic suggesting that individuals have little or no resistance to crime should they learn serial rape from others. That is, it ignores individual decisions to remain crime free. Then, too, there is a gap between attitudes and behavior. Furthermore, social learning neglects the role of unconscious social processes in shaping nonconformity. For instance, new attitudes repress, replace, or reshape old attitudes depending upon how you wish to phase it. Lastly, not all individuals learn anything even from the best teachers. Many individuals have priorities that may not include learning. Thus, learning is not always accomplished even when it is on the agenda of a student (this part I know well)! Therefore, learning crime seems to be a convenient yet an inadequate conclusion about serial rape.

Subculture

Subculture theorists review police reports of rapists and largely conclude that predatory rape is motivated by a subculture theory of violence. This perspective finds some merit within the social learning perspectives as it suggests that individuals in a subculture of violence learn the techniques of serial rape from their environment.[20] Perhaps this idea implies that if an individual is socialized in a ghetto the likelihood that he will

---

19. Albert Bandura (1973) presents the strongest argument on social learning. But, Lee Ellis (1989) also offers an in-depth discussion specifically on rapists.

20. For a closer look see Menachem Amir (1971) although his work is dated and highly controversial.

engage in violent crime is greater than an individual who had not been socialized in a ghetto. Yet, subculture perspectives neglect to consider that many individuals have been raised in affluence across America, and they are rapists too.

Revenge and Sex

Some writers suggest that while sex could be the primary motivation in date-rape, they say, however, that domination and control motivates predatory rapes. Then, too, there exists an idea that stranger rapists use sexual violence as a method of revenge and punishment while other rapists use it to gain access to unwilling women.[21] These advocates add that rapists exhibit compulsive masculinity, a common characteristic of some subcultures, and hold stereotypical beliefs about rape. Yet, there are a few theorists who hint that some serial rapists may want sexual intimacy from their victims, but these writers claim that this idea is not a primary cause of serial rape for any rapist.

Summary

In summary, there are many claims about predatory rape from individuals who have never committed the crime. With so many convincing and in some cases eloquent theories about the causes of predatory rape, it's hard to imagine that some of them are inaccurate. For instance, a continuum exists with motivating factors ranging from cultural

---

21. For a discussion on date-rape see Eugene Kanin (1985). For discussions on revenge and punishment see Diana Scully and Joseph Marolla (1984). For an in-death review of sexual intimacy as a motivation for serial rape see both Scully (1990) and Catherine MacKinnon (1987).

aspects of inequality and exploitation to biologically inclined suggestions explaining that violence and anger are behavioral objectives with DNA markers and neurohormonal factors as major motivators. Other claims suggest that social learning theories show violence as instrumental as opposed to an objective. Some writers say that a subculture perspective buttresses revenge, punishment, and compulsive masculinity leading to predatory rape. While others indicate that sexual drives could in a few cases be responsible for a few serial rape attacks. One problem with many of these theories is that they advocate specific methods of victim response to attackers–submit; another problem when accepting inadequate theory relates to insufficient crime control–custody. Herein lays the major problems or opportunities, if you will, connected with those perspectives. Maybe it's time to hear from the experts-by-experience–the criminals themselves in order to understand offender motive, victim avoidance, and crime control techniques.

CHAPTER 4

Findings

Admitting Serial Rape

Thirteen incarcerated offenders enrolled in a university course entitled Sociology of Crime were trained as student-interviewers to help conduct this study. This study was comprised of 61 offenders who were incarcerated at a maximum custody penitentiary.[22]

Among the 61 participants, 3% (2) of them admitted to at least fifty rapes each or 100; 5% (3) offenders admitted to at least twenty-five rapes each or 75; 13% (8) admitted to ten rapes each or total of 80, 26% of them admitted to two rapes each or 32; and 40% (24) admitted to one rape each or 24 rapes (see Table 1). The remaining 5% (3) offenders reported that their rape convictions "were a case of mistaken identity," while another 3 said they had never committed rape, however all 6 of them had been convicted for sexual assault and each offered descriptions of predatory rape during their interviews. Therefore, based on the responses of 61 offenders, a conservative guess is that the sample attempted to at least 319 predatory rapes or an average of 5.2 rapes per participant.

---

22. see Appendix 2 for specific details about the methodology used. See Appendix 4 for sample, date collection, and typology.

Stop! Let's realize something that might be uncomfortable. Men who commit predatory rape don't always see their heinous crimes as an offense; when called upon to discuss their criminal activities, they may give only those experiences they considered illegal. Other times, they simply lose track of their criminal lifestyles. So, how accurate are those past unimportant events? One guess is that they aren't, but another guess is that collectively this group underestimated their attacks and probably committed closer to four times the number they discussed. That might put their real number of attacks around 1276 or 21 each.[23] Once these men are released, (and most of them have been at the writing of this book) they will commit more violent crimes including serial rape largely due to their previous lifestyles prior to their incarceration and due in part to their experiences at prison.[24]

Table 1		Admitting Serial Rape			(N=61)		
Not Sure	Never/ Denied	Never/ Mistaken Identity	Once	Twice	10/More	25/More	50/More
3%	5%	5%	40%	26%	13%	5%	3%

* percents rounded

23. For a life time of crime, since the average age was 32 at the time of the interviews and most of the descriptions of the participants characterized what appeared to be criminal lifestyle experiences at 21, two rapes a year for 10 years might be closer to the truth.

24 Both male and female nonviolent offenders incarcerated in prison tend to assimilate the norms, values, and violence of a prison and depending on their prison time served, once released, most will engage in a variety of violent crimes due to their prison experiences. For a closer look see Stevens 1994, 1996, 1998.

Motives of Serial Rapists

When offender accounts were examined for motive leading to preda-tory attacks, clear patterns emerged: 42% (25) of the offenders largely characterized sexual contact as their primary goal for their attacks on females or what I call lust (see Table 2). Fifteen percent (9) of the offend-ers revealed that their predatory attacks were encouraged by the victims themselves or what the participants called "righteous rape," while 3% (2) of the offenders blamed friends or peers as their reasons for their attacks. Another 8% (5) of the offenders suggested control/anger as their motivat-ing force bringing them to serial rape, while 13% (8) of the rapists described supremacy over their victims as their goal. Sixteen percent (10) of the participants described fantasy as the motivating force behind their attacks, and 3% (2) of the respondents presented unclear descriptions about their motivators.

Lust

Lustful objectives were described by many of the predatory rapists, although some of the offenders largely described lust as their only goal. Specifically, 42% (25) of the accounts described what I call lustful charac-teristics answering a question as to why these men sexually attacked females whom they had never met. To determine lust as a primary goal, the statements of the participants were carefully examined for indicators of a sexual nature, selection techniques (Chapter 6), and use of force (Chapter 7). For instance, some of the typical remarks leading to this con-clusion include the following.[25]

> I watched her ass…and I watched her eyes…I got this chill
> running down my legs to the accelerator (of my car). Henry
> Watching this cunt walk at the pool, stoked my insides. A itch
> the size of a horse licked my dick. John

There was something about the way she looked. I wanted to see if she looked the same way when her ol'e man was humping her. Barry

It's simple, man, I love pussy.[26] Carmen

Account after account suggested that licentiously driven offenders had time prior to their attacks to make conscious assessments about their victims. That is, the gauges used to determine lust as a primary motive included both statements of a sexual nature and indications that offenders had opportunities to make assessments of the victims prior to their attacks. For example:

The ol'e guy saw me and I was polite. I helped them into the elevator and touched her tits and ass while holding her up. Not bad, I remember thinking. I decided I'd screw her if I could..... He passed out in the living room, and I poured her into bed. I think she pushed me away, but I held her hands with one hand and pulled her skirt up. Her cunt smelled, but it welcomed my dick and it seemed forever but I finally came [ejaculated]. He

---

25. The statements used by the predators were not edited. Their explicit and vulgar language is neither encouraged nor appropriate for most of us; and, I wish to apologize for any discomfort you might experience when reading some of these pages. Most grammatical inconsistencies may be the error of the participants interviewed rather than the error of the writer. However, to edit their comments to fit what we consider acceptable language, might change the meaning of what the offenders have to say. All names used were fictitious.

26. When the lustful offenders spoke about their victims before and many times after their attacks, they distinguished their victims as: honeys, babes, sweet things, cute, sexy creatures, dolls, young sweeties, killer babes, lovelies, and pretties. That is, they referred to females as objects of endearment and rarely used vulgar adjectives to describe them.

suddenly appeared and started hitting me. I shoved him. He kept on com'en. When I ran out, I forgot my shoes.

I was watching this babe peddling her bike. She looks good, and I was hungry. She's real young. I wanted that cunt. I knew she couldn't stop me. I ran along and ask if she saw my little sis. She stops, and I smell her sweat. I wan'na taste it. We walked together talk'en 'bout my sis till we passed a field. So I took that little babe and made her chew my dick. Billy

This tight look'en girl was fumbling with her keys, tr'en to get into her fal'en down shed [in her yard]. I saw her from the street. She wore a nightee that I could almost see through. The way she moved made my rocks shake. I had to have her. So I pretended to look for my dog. She was much older than I thought. She like was polite but bitchy, ya know what I mean? Told her some'en like, sorry lady. She goes, yea like get lost. Now I don't give a fuck, ya know. I reach for her neck. Fuck you, I goes, and drag her inside the fuck'en shed. Okay, now put your mouth on this or some'en like that, I goes. But I was too scared to get hard. I ran. Cidel

Other descriptions characterized by lustful offenders which distinguished them from the other serial rapist categories were that their descriptions often revealed a preference for vaginal penetration; they rarely used vulgar adjectives to describe victims; and they were intense men who characterized emotional feelings for their victims. Some of those emotional-charged comments came before their sexual attack and some came after it. For example:

One time this honey was asleep but I just looked till I…Ric

[after the attack]…kissed her. Robby

Be still…held her like aaa…liked that sexy creature for a moment.

But she [the victim] made me so horny, I went home and screwed my ol'e lady to death. I member…something though…screw'en my ol'e lady…I 'membered that little babe's eyes. They were mmm, pretties real pretties and gentle like. Collin

Lust is not a new idea as Catherine MacKinnon and Diana Scully found, too, when they studied the question of stranger rape. Yet neither writer suggests that sexual motivation was the primary goal for most serial rapists. But, as evidenced by the above descriptions, many predatory rapists are driven by their desire to have immediate sexual contact with females; they most often prefer sexual intercourse with their victims, and they are often emotionally concerned with their pray. It should be noted that lustful offenders' selection techniques were more focused on easy-prey selection techniques as explained in Chapter 6, and they rarely used force to subdue their victims before, during, or after their sexual attacks as explained in more detail in Chapter 7.

Righteous Rape

Of 61 predatory rape cases, 15% (9) of the descriptions characterized what those rapists called righteous rape as a primary motive for their attacks. These nine offenders said that their victims produced "the circumstances and the conditions" for rape by striking a "silent deal" with them, one rapist explained. That is, some predators (and defense lawyers) often blame victims for the attacks.

Look, from the perspective of an offender, it's better to blame someone else for the crimes he commits than himself. That way, an offender doesn't sound as bad as his behavior looks nor does he have to accept the responsibility for his actions. Why not tag a person he already knows is an easy target? In fact, most of these offenders distinguished themselves from the other categories of motives through their use of easy-prey target techniques as discussed in Chapter 6 and as predators who used little if any physical force before, during, or after their attack as discussed in Chapter 7. An example of this type of thinking can be illustrated in Wild Bill's statement.

> I was mind'en my own friggen business, do'en some real good shit [drugs] near the swings, when this sweet white babe shots her parts my's way and smiles. Ya give me some blow [drugs], and I'll show ya a good time, she says.

Wild Bill sets the hook for us when he revealed that supposedly, she, made a deal with him. Maybe she had, but part of the deal from her perspective certainly didn't include rape. Wild Bill suggested that he was an innocent bystander! After all, he picked the place to get distribute drugs, and surely he knew some of the types of individuals who frequented the area. But, as Wild Bill presented more of his story, he revealed his true mission.

> She looks good, real nice. See, man, I wants this 'hole, so I let her help herself. She did'em and walks, laughing—telling (her) friends she made me. I catch her later on a back street and lay the 'hole down. I goes som'en like you owe. She don't act nothing like she's expecting it. I knew she'd be sweet. How'd I know tat' hole was twelve! But I had the right to that snatch. She gets exactly what she asks for, my big dick. Wild Bill

What these offenders are saying is an attempt to justify both their method of coercion and the sexual attacks. That is, they are not guilty by reason of circumstance. It seems that righteous rape accounts could easily fit lustful rape motive accounts as Wild Bill's aim is directed towards sexual contact. He gave drugs for sex in the first place. He's done this before and knew the game! Blaming a victim isn't the cause of the attack.

There are differences in the accounts of the righteous rapists and the accounts of lustful rapists concerning their primary motive. First, those individuals who blamed their victims used vulgar adjectives to describe their victims such as 'holes, whores, and bitches. Second, the cases of the righteous rapists described both vaginal penetration and oral sex; and third, in the righteous cases, unlike the lust accounts, they seem to characterized justification of their crimes. For example:

> I got drunk one night with this piece of shit bitch I worked with. We started making it in her car. I went down on her and she touched me like she enjoyed it. She got me so frigg'en hard that I'd have a stroke if she didn't make me come. I told her she'd better suck me off or else. Fuck it, I said, I was horny, I just pushed it into her bitch-pit and came as I did. It was fuck'en what's happen'n man...Hampton
>
> I believe it's clear where Ben is going with his remarks by suggesting that she enjoyed their sexual activity. He is inferring that his victim is now obligated to go as far as he wanted her too. Notice, I'm saying as far as he wanted her to go! Yet, as Ben continues his narrative, he reports that he knew his attack was rape, but he solicits sympathy trying to sell someone on the idea he became a victim of both the victim and the state. Narration presented by the inmate-interviewee.

Continuing along this thought, blaming rape victims for rape is suggestive of an awareness of cultural ideals in that rape is an inappropriate sexual activity. To be inappropriate translates to cultural deviance. Therefore, in order to be a conformist, or one of the good guys, an offender must place the blame on others. To say, I attacked a woman because I wanted to have sex with her, might be the comment of a man who doesn't care what others think or an offender who is not up for parole. Righteous rapists apparently care what others think, right to their method of their sexual assault!

Then, too, some psychologists like to dig into a rapist's past and explain the blame from those experiences of an offender.[27] But the truth of the matter is as one of the rapists said about most of the women he attacked, "She was so sexy! I couldn't stop. I'd eat her shit to fuck her every day— every way, man." Because his victims were attractive, it follows that it was her fault that he raped her! So let me ask a question: why didn't he date her or court her or marry her in order to have sex with her since Marvin, like the other righteous rapists claimed that he would do anything to have sex with his victims? In what way might Marvin's early childhood experiences have something to do with his behavior 20 some years later? The unique thing about humans is that they are constantly changing; and humans evaluate and re-evaluate their social environments, ideals, and experiences all the time. Truth is, most of us develop of our own social meanings and social realities and what was true yesterday, isn't true today. Look at our divorce rate as an example; we loved'em, we adored'em yesterday and today, we want someone else! Many children have had abusive experiences and they aren't raping and killing.

In sum, both lustful and righteous offenders characterizes sexual intimacy as their primary objective for their predatory attacks. They individually and collectively described similar methods of finding and subduing their victims (see Chapters 6 & 7), and preferred sexual intercourse with their victims.

---

27. For instance, Ronald Holmes (1991: pp. 79) likes to rely on severe physical punishment by their dominating, sadistic, and castrating mothers as motivators of rape.

Peer Rape

Oddly enough, 3% (2) of the offenders' accounts characterized friendship as an agent of cause for rape. "I had no choice, I ran with bad company," Tyrone said. Righteous rapists blamed victims, peer rapists blamed friends for their criminally. For instance:

> Michael is a 24 year old black male serving a sentence of 28 years for his participation in a gang rape which took place in 1987. Michael admits his participation but pled not guilty, and maintains he is without responsibility for the incident stating that he was forced into it by two co-defendants. He indicated his co-defendants questioned his masculinity and called him chicken as well as threatened him with physical violence. He had to prove himself. They were at the playground and decided on a 13 year old who liked to hang with us and thought she was some kind'a groupie. An inmate-interviewer reported.
>
> Bernard and his partner went camping. A woman was hiking along the trail. Bernard's friend told him that this was the opportunity he was waiting for. He grabbed the woman. He tore off her clothes and told him to take his off. Then he forced her into oral sex with Bernard. When Bernard hesitated, he called him chicken shit. Bernard noticed that his partner was not hard, but had sex with her anyway. She was skinny and didn't turn Bernard on. He was shaking and afraid of getting caught. His partner whispered that we should kill her. Bernard said no. Having a partner is like being drunk, you feel braver and stronger. An inmate-interviewer reported.

Explaining peer motives is similar to the above discussion about righteous rapists—peer pressure is an excuse. However, it is not clear as to what really motivated these offenders when they commented the crime of rape.

One safe thought is that sexual desire plays a role in their decisions to rape and/or possibly their virility. Perhaps, it is convenient that their friends forced them into sex with an unknown person. Righteous and peer rapists bring to mind ideas of Stanford Lyman and Marvin Scott (1989). These writers suggest that excuses are designed to relieve the offender of criminal responsibility and justifications are designed to neutralize their act and its consequences.[28] In applying this idea to serial rapists, some offenders think they should not be punished for rape because they had not committed a crime. It is like the prostitute who thinks she is a social worker or a drug pusher who thinks he is supplying people with items they want. In some of my recent studies, I find that motives are accepted justifications for present, future, or past programs or acts, but those justifications relate to immediate or current experiences more than past experiences.[29] That is, in an effort to fit in, some rapists are using present ideals or attitudes to explain historical accounts in their past. It makes sense as these rapists, are saying what they think are currently socially approved ideals and expectations to explain their past actions. It could be that some rapists think it fashionable to blame their victims.

---

28. For an in-depth look at this discussion see Stanford Lyman and Marvin Scott (1989).

29. For example, in a study of 419 inmates at Attica in New York, findings showed that attitudes are descriptions of feelings and have little if any relevance to previous behavior. An implication arising from the data of that test is that scholarly explanations of offenders are descriptions of behavior rather than "truths" about offender attitudes. See Stevens (1995). Also, see C. Wright Mills (1945).

Table 2	Motive Categories	(N=61)
Category	Percent	Number
Lust	42%	25
Righteous	15%	9
Peer	3%	2
Control/Anger	8%	5
Supremacy	13%	8
Fantasy	16%	10
Other	3%	2
Total	100%	61

* percents rounded therefore column does not equal 100%

** represents not sures, never/denied, and never/mistake identity

CHAPTER 5

Control, Supremacy, and Fantasy

Control and Anger

Eight percent (6) of the accounts characterized control and anger as a primary objective leading to serial rape. In these accounts, more violence was described by the respondents than necessary to accomplish rape. That is, violence was used even after the victim submitted and during the entire encounter, illustrating the use of violence for its own sake. The individuals who pursued violence reported great degrees of anger, too. In these cases, the rapes were described as incidental activity secondary to the violence powered by their anger. For example

> I was pissed with my wife…looking for action. But I didn't wan'a fuck, and I didn't want to hear screams. So, if I found some bitch who was dead or unconscious even, hypothetically that is, then she can't scream and sure as hell can't say no like my frigg'en wife. I saw this fine looking broad in the parking lot carrying a load of food with a little kid hanging on to her dress. I pushed her into the car and grabbed the kid by the throat. I slid in on top of her and said to the bitch, it you ain't a good little girl, I'd kill your kid. She said something to me that I didn't understand so I slammed her with my free hand. I told her, I want you to suck my cock. She started to but the kid won't shut

up so I shook it. And she was crying really loud. I ran. Jake. Note: never arrested for this crime.

Control and anger seem to flow from each word Jake offered. But, Jake tended to describe a minimal amount of force in comparison to Bones who offered a typical control and anger perspective.

> I picked up this chick at some rat hole [bar]. We got in my car and started petting and petting. She stopped said she should'a been with her husband. Imagine, she's go'en down (oral sex] on me and now I'm not good enough for her. Fuck her! I pulled her hair almost off her skull and shove my beer bottle in her pussy as far as it could go. You should'a seen her face, when I pulled her out of the car with her hair in one hand and the bottle in t'a other! She found out who was in charge, and it ain't her. I pulled the bottle out of her cunt and slammed her a homer [rape] while l held her by the ha in I think she was off the ground the whole time. She was sort of not with it, but I made her finish me off in her mouth. Bones. Note: never arrested for this crime

Control and anger seem to be related in these narratives. This interpretation is consistent with the perspective that sexuality is only the means of expressing the aggressive needs and feelings that operate in the offender and underlie his assault.

Supremacy

Thirteen percent (8) of the participants described their forcible rape attacks with an emphasis upon unnecessary violence before, during, and after the attack. I refer to these individuals as supremacy rapists. Fact is, these respondents characterized anger in their chronicles wailing into a stone of rage to gain victim submission. Sadly, their rage continued long past victim subjugation and in some cases—long past a victim's demise. Rage blinds their violence, and sex is their alibi to exercise it. They seem to have little interest in sex itself as evidenced by the Jerry's example:

> Me and a lot of other kids were in this temporary foster house for abused kids. The daughter of the house-parents was always bossing us around, so one day that was it! I threw her on the bed. We fought for a while. I won. And put it to that little fucken whore. After that I forced into sex when ever I had noth'en to do and made her come up to my room to spend the night…I told her I'd tell her parents that she was screw'en all of us and would get pregnant if she told. A few times I forced her to have oral sex with some of the other guys. I think she was like 10. This went on a few weeks till they found me a foster home. I showed the little bitch 'bout sex. Got their dog up stairs once and made her watch when I made the little fucker shot its wad by pulling its meat. She said she liked it. I told her if she said anything that that dog was gonna hump her and then bite her friggen nipples. Jerry

Sexual contact played an insignificant role; what took precedence for this rapist was the punishment they inflicted on their victims. These rapists demonstrated little regard for their victims as human beings. Like other violence fiends, they transcend humanity—especially the humanity of their victims. Their victims are punching bags designed to absorb their rage and their urges. Manny's descriptions of predatory rape below revealed each of these characteristics and brought to light other characteristics of the supremacy rapist:

> I followed her to her car. I looked like I was getting in the car next to hers checking everything out. When she opened her door…was busy being it was Christmas time, I pushed inside

and forced her to the floor. She was cry'en so I kicked her and told her to shut the fuck up. Bout a mile out of town I pulled into a abandoned lot. I grabbed her by the hair. You suck this bitch...She must'a been afraid cuz she crabbed right there. Fuck'en aaaa, man. I rubbed her fuck'en face in it like the fuck-'en whore dog she is. Drove around town for awhile; She didn't run or cry or nothin'. At McDonalds, I told her to go down on me but the fuck'en shit smelled, man...finally said screw it, and put it in her right there in the lot but covered her face with her skirt. She was cold the whole time. I pissed on her....kept some of her I.D. and spent all her money. I told her that if she fingers me, I'd get her...Drove by the cunt's house and watched...Kept that bitch the rest of the night...punched her ass...Driving down the friggen highway (interstate), she passed out from the shit I was push'en down her throat (drugs and liquor); that's when I did it (pushed her out on to the interstate). Sam

Closer inspection of the above accounts suggests that supremacy rapists used sex as a devise to inflict degradation and punishment on their victims. Individuals who commit the crime of rape do so as an effort to deal with the unresolved and the conflictual aspects of their lives. Supremacy rape is an expression of power and assertion of the rapist's strength and manhood. these writers claim. These rapists are people who have taken woman-hating to its furthest possible point—the actual acting out of the body that some men do only in fantasy.[30]

---

30. Also, see Les Sussman and Sally Bordwell (1981).

Fantasy Rape

Sixteen percent (10) of the accounts suggested that the respondents were attempting to fulfill imaginary goals bordering unreality or invented scenarios. That is, these individuals were primarily trying to regain some imaginary goal that had been part of their past, or so they described in their accounts. Sexual contact was described as an event that helped fulfill those goals. Therefore, would it be prudent to suggest that sex may not be a goal and in many cases, unnecessary. For example, Martin said:

> In my head I think about women in precarious positions. I devise shit like spreading her legs on a rack. I think about hurting'em and tak'en in their cries for help. But, I don't do any of that shit. I tell'em once—okay, bitch you know what I want. This could go hard or easy on you. It's up to you. Most of the time, they put out that fast and usual say shit like, don't kill me. Please, don't kill me! Hell, I don't want'a kill'em, I just want'a screw'em. Martin

Martin conveyed that he was motivated by his ideas that he had created. However, other accounts described more than visions and characterized behavior showing how the participant turned his thoughts into criminally violent behavior to fulfill his objectives. For instance, Henry, in the following account, explained his illusion:

> When I was little, my uncle used to baby sit me. I used to spy on him and his girl friend when they had sex. The way they went through the motions was perfect. I wanted to be just like them. Henry

However, as Henry revealed more of his experiences, his thoughts led to behavior suggesting that he was attempting to bring those illusions to reality.

> So when I was with girls I pretend I was him (his uncle) and they were her. I'd tell'em how I wanted them to lay or form their body. I'd masturbate on'em. When I was a punk, I d break into homes and force old fuck'en folks there into venous positions and masturbate. Sometimes…I pretended I was my uncle's slut. I made sure some of those folks pulled their chains (masturbated) on me. Henry

Unfortunately, the behavior described by Henry takes violent turns and we are left with the idea that Henry wanted to pursue his goal, no matter the cost as the benefits of his deed far outweighed the consequences of his crime. It seems that all serial rapists pretty weigh the benefits of their crimes as opposed to the consequences of their behavior.[31] Apparently, criminals like the those described above have a finite plan which brings to mind offenders like Edward Gein who danced in the moonlight wearing the face, the hair, the breasts, and the vaginas of his victims.[32]

"Other" Rape

"Other" or unclear motives were suggested by 3 percent (2) of the participants; however, the example given seems to complement a power perspective and/or a cultural inequality view. For example:

> My guy says he sees a check in the parking lot that he knows will love his ass once they're together. Inside, he goes up to her

---

31. Also, see Gottfredson and Hirschi (1989) who hold a similar perspective about career criminals.

32. For a closer look see Gollmar, R. H. (1981). Edward Gein. NY: Windsor Publishing.

and if she own a certain car and gives her the tag (license plate) number. He says that these babes always sound like they're doing him a favor by talking to him, but he always has a upper hand because he's smarter. He describes something on the seat, and asks about the small animal socked inside that looks sick. She runs to the car. Inside looking for the cat, ho goes, I own your ass, bitch. You can get hurt or it will be over soon. He sat on her chess and pulls his meat (masturbates) in her face. He wants to start quick and end quick. When he shots, it goes in her mouth. He splits. An interviewer explained.

Does a closer review of the data suggest that the description can characterize lustful intentions on the part of the rapist?

Summary

In summary, from the previous chapter, the data suggest that 62 percent (38) of the respondents (lust, righteous rape, peer, and other) characterized lustful intentions as their primary goal leading to their sexual attacks. For some, their lust led them to believe that their victims promoted the circumstances and the conditions for rape. In this chapter, the data show that less often then expected, offenders raped in order to gain control over their victims and fewer rapists yet, raped for total domination over their victims. Then, too, some of the descriptions of the rapists characterized fantasy rape which was fueled by lustful imaginations.

Some experts say that most predatory rapists are violent and angry men, and I think we can see from the above statements typifying violent offenders that they offer some valuable insight. Yet, they fail to recognize that many men are angry, and many men have reason to be angry with many experiences including their experiences with women. What also comes to light is that the rage of some these rapists is tied directly to their conscious and cool decisions producing grotesque acts as they move toward their primary objective—masterful superiority of their victims. One question that needs to be answered is: are these offenders in control of their own actions? Are they in control of their own rage? Can they turn it off and can they turn it on? In a word, yes. Emotions such as anger and rage are devises used by some offenders to manipulate others support this idea. Therefore, some descriptions of violent hateful men are inadequate especially when those descriptions show that some deep seated mysterious mechanism triggers these hateful men into action. The actions described by the rapists in this study did not support any idea that their actions were tied to some mysterious beam from the past or for that matter, a beam from the planet Mungo.

It becomes clear that no single pattern of rape represents all serial rapists. When we think of rape, many people visualize a sex-starved mad-man waiting with a weapon for his prey. Despite the consistency in the stereotype, characterizing stranger rape requires diversity. There is no one type of stranger rapist just as there is no one type of stranger rape victim. Yet, most violent offenders like serial rapists, weigh the benefits of their crimes as opposed to the consequences arising from them. Thus, most criminals can not be deterred from committing crimes of violence because they may be apprehended more often or because capital punishment is exercised more often. Thus, their own destruction is the only way of eliminating that individual as a future rapists.

CHAPTER 6

Selection Techniques

Victim Selection

Which females do predators attack most often? Attractive women? Young girls? Athletic females? When the answers of the chronic offenders were placed into categories to answer that question, the most frequently mentioned characteristic of victim selection wasn't looks or age but vulnerability. That is, when predators thought a female could not or would not resist an attack and an opportunity prevailed by circumstance or manipulation, they attacked regardless of her appearance, age, or physical condition. The following categories[33] (see Table 3) arose from the data of the offenders: easy prey; random; situational; and unclear.

---

33. Before going on, I should share that in an earlier study I included two categories not shown above: victim attractive and victim age. There are two things I want to say about that. One, I was wrong and after reworking my earlier efforts, found the error of my ways. Two, the error was that many of the statements which at first reflected victim attractiveness or victim age were perceived in relationship to one of the other categories. That is, less attractive women who were perceived as easy prey were more desirable than more attractive women who were not perceived as easy prey. Therefore, a victim's vulnerability, randomness, and/or situation were more important than looks, age, or her condition. Therefore, being fair with you, I streamlined my work for your convenience.

TABLE 3	TARGET SELECTION METHODS	(N=61)
	NUMBER	PERCENTS
EASY PREY	42	69%
RANDOM	7	11%
SITUATIONAL	9	15%
NOT SURE	3	5%

Easy Prey

Forty-two of the 61 rapists (69%) characterized victim vulnerability in their descriptions as the best reason to sexually attack a female or what I call easy prey. Easy prey specifically refers to females whom the offenders perceived as vulnerable. "Hell, the easiest (prey) are the ones out of it or old, I mean old," said Kelly. Just how easy is easy? Below are two typical accounts describing how offenders selected there "out of it" or "old" victims to sexually attack.

> I was parking my car in the condo lot where I was renting. This older couple pulled in. They were drunk…Dwayne
>
> I was working maintenance at a hospital in Florida. I'd keep my eye on the women patients and every so often go into their rooms when they were out of it and screw'em. I got caught but said it happened only once. They didn't want the publicity so they fired me and never called the cops. I knew they'd do that cause it happened before at a old people's home where I worked. Hurbert (Note: never arrested or convicted for any sexual crime)

Young Girls as Easy Prey

There were disagreements between the participants about which females were easy prey. Some claimed that "the easiest (prey) is young girls," said Hank. For instance, he offered the following typical narrative about victim selection:

> I stopped at this chain joint for lunch somewhere between Knoxville and Ashville....I ordered and this real cute girl caught my eye. She must'a been with her folks. Maybe she was 14, maybe 12. She saw me grin and smiled back. That's the tip off that I can have her. (When) she headed for the bathroom...Hank

Hank went into detail about his attack, an attack suggesting that if his victim was older or more experienced, things might have turned out different. Age and/or inexperience were determining factors. He continued with:

> I made a line for it (bathroom) too real slow like, look'en to the ground so not to cause no stir. She went in. I went in. Someone was in a stall, but no one was outside. She didn't say a word when I grabbed her arm. I frowned and went shhh, don't want to hurt ya, I says. I moved her into the end stall. I guess I was scared cause I couldn't get in her. She was real dry and I was seat'en on the stool with her on my lap. The woman in the stall finished up. I pushed her to the floor and put it [his penis] in her mouth. Don't ya spit it out when I come, I said real low. And when I came, it leaked over her lips. Cleaned it off with toilet paper and kissed her. Hank

Another offender, Eddy, characterized how a younger or less experienced female became his victim once he determined her vulnerably.

Watching this shit-flick at the movies but watch'en these young sweeties a few rows down. Each time they leave, they're gone for 10 minutes or so. Probably screw'en around somewhere. When they leave, I waltz up next to the one they left behind. I smile but she doesn't look at me. I put my knife to her stomach. Put your mouth on it, I say tak'en my dick out of my pants. She hesitated but I push the knife into her more. She covers my dick and I could almost get off like that. Went into the john and yanked off in a stall watching these guys pee. Left that movie place and never went back. Eddy (Note: never prosecuted).

How can perceived vulnerability of children be related to easy prey? One explanation can be that younger females may demonstrate yielding cues to predators through their behavior, in part, due to their caretakers who assume that their children are more responsible and mentally older then they are. Look, many parents treat their children like friends and have adult expectations for them.[34]

A analysis of affluent middle class children shows that they tend to have more freedom than lower class children since their caretakers tend to ignore or tend pass to others (i.e. psychiatric hospitals or councilors) essential discipline and guidance which children require to develop inter-personal skills to deal with predators.[35] Therefore, children tend to rely upon their limited experiences and unlimited choices when confronted by strangers perhaps resulting in a belief that they are in control and that no harm will come to them. What some children fail to comprehend is that

---

34. This view is consistent with some of my earlier work suggesting that parents, especially middle class parents, tend to encourage their children to demand their rights as long as those rights do not interfere with the life-styles of their parents. See Stevens (1988). Also, see Frederick Elkin and Gerald Handel (1984).

35. Also see Ira Schwartz (1989) who argues that parents at every socioeconomic level demand that law enforcement, school counselors, and social workers both guide and discipline their children for them.

they are no longer dealing with people who are accountable for their actions. Additionally, as evidenced by Hank and Eddy's comments, predators know how to use childhood independence against their victims.

Middle Class Females as Easy Prey Victims

However, women in the financial district of large cities acquiescence to predators, too. For example, Randall a 31 year old black man convicted of armed robbery (only one victim testified against him in a sexual misconduct charge), had "sixty or seventy naive women" who were his victims. Before incarceration, he regularly scouted the financial districts of several cities for sex and money. He would lean on his shiny late model Cadillac wearing an expensive suit. As "hip well-dressed" woman walked by, he would smile and ask for information. He said that when a woman answered his question and "glances down or looks away," he knew she could be victimized. A friend of Randall claimed that lower class women would tell him to "go fuck himself and stare him down. But patty (white Irish] girls are trained to be polite, but look's away from a black buck like him."

As I have suggested earlier, women tend to internalize messages that devalue femaleness from an early age suggesting that they are irrational, immoral, emotional, dependent, and submissive. Continuing along this thought, aren't these predators describing a search for females who have been socially trained to yield to males? Once discovered, pleasant conversation is pursued and intimidation is used, if necessary, to frighten her into obedience if she does not comply with his sexual demands at first. Randall is clearly a typical example of a rapist who rarely attacked females whom he perceives as street-wise.

Occupational Tracking and Easy Prey

Part of the ease of victims encountered in the streets by predators is due to the early childhood training of many middle class females who are too independent or in this case, were socially trained as supportive individuals responding to the needs of others; and partly due to occupational tracking of females into helper roles like nurses, teachers, and social workers. Submissive roles at home and in the work place are routinely demanded of females. Another way of explaining women's obedience is that predators manipulate "helping women" into vulnerable situations by drawing upon their helper objectives. For instance:

Saw this doll alone run'en down the road. I watched her ass jump up and down before I passed her, and I watched her eyes squint through my mirror. I got this chill running down my legs to the accelerator. The next thing was, could it happen without a fight? I pulled my van on the side of the road and fiddled under the hood. Soon I saw her coming towards me. I put my knuckle on the manifold and burned the fuck out of'em. I screamed and she came a'run'en. I told her my first aid kit was in the glove box. She climbed in. That was it. Do it or else, I say. She didn't fuss or nothing. Edmond

I follow some cute babe from the parking lot at a mall....I ask her bout the small animal locked in the car....it looks sick or something. We almost run to. Petey

Ease and the benefit of the crime seem to be the life work of these offenders.

Shoppers as Easy Prey

Other selection processes have to do with how a shopper "carries" herself or demeanor, the offenders argue. For instance, one rapist said he observed how women respond to others as shoppers at food stores. Women who bumped into other shoppers and were "overly apologetic, were dead give-aways." Other typical descriptions follow:

> If she's not watching what's happening all around her, then doesn't know how to handle herself, how to use the things around her to hurt me or get me caught. Jona
>
> Whether we're talk'en bout a robbery or sex, depends on the mark (victim]. See, if they're going to hurt me, no way. When these broads are awake (alert, they] tell ya to 'get bent' right out when ya approach'em. Brent

In sum, the nonverbal cues or messages a female seems to send apparently has much to do with how predators perceive her defense attitudes. "If she's dizzy say at K Mart's checkout, it means she probably won't make a decision to strike back till it's too late, if she's going to do it at all," claimed our food store predator. Nonverbal communication is often an honest mirror of the thoughts of human beings, and it adds a whole new dimension to the communication process. Apparently, chronic offenders rely on their skill of reading nonverbal cues as part of their decision-making process to attack or not to attack a victim. But, let's face it, fear entrepreneurs and politically correct scholars both promote and reinforce the fear of rape and a learned helplessness among females. Females learn that they can not win against assailants. They simply follow the advice of those they trust and give in. That makes me as equally angry as some of these rapists in this study!

Females Who Decrease Their Defense Capabilities

Of course, predatory rapists do not always succeed as evidenced by government statistics, but the more they attack helpless "appearing" women, the greater their chances of success. "It's a numbers game," claimed Bubba. Women decrease their defense capabilities by placing themselves in dangerous situations-situations that do not go unnoticed. For instance:

> I watched this old bitch at a party get high. I've seen her around campus a few times and was interested. She was messing with everybody. What a tease! I danced with her a few times and suggested we go into one of the bedrooms. Kiss'en, hug'en, touch'en, ya know the scene. When I was ready to do her, she goes, no man, not that. I'm married. F…you, I says. She pushed me away but she was so high she couldn't get up enough push. Bamm, I'm in her and at first she's struggling a little then she got in to it. Man, she shook her ass so much I thought I'd lose my dick in her. She called campus police in the morning and they asked me about it. I told'em what I'm telling you and they said she didn't have a case. I agree, the bitch! I ain't seen her around anymore. Her ol'e man probably made her drop out. Serves her right. Glen

In sum, 69% of the descriptions of the rapists characterized easy prey as their primary criterion prior to sexually attacking a female.

Random

Prior to any sexual attacks, 7 (11%) of the offenders revealed that while they were engaged in another activity like robbery or criminal trespass, they came upon their victims by chance. In this sense, it appears that the offenders said that they were not actively seeking victims. However, in most of the descriptions they suggested that almost immediately upon discovering the presence of a female, they altered their earlier activities and assaulted her. The following typical statements characterized the chance victim selection descriptions of the sample.

> We broke into this hospital drug store…I ducked into a room where this chick is out cold. I saw in a movie where this guy gets in a hospital bed and when they check, they don't see nothing but the patient. So, in I go (under the covers with his victim). Paully
>
> Each morn'en bout 9:00 to 12:00 when I'm on the move, I check motels out cause that's when the maids are clea'em up…I get lucky and find a key. Bout dinner time, I'd come back and chec'em out. I'd make people for small things. One time, this honey's asleep…Stinger

What these rapists are saying is that any female could have been victimized regardless of her appearance, age, or condition. That is, every female is a potential victim of a serial rapist if she happens to become part of his environment and perceives her as vulnerable and/or coheres her into submission through intimidation and/or violence. For example:

> One of my old partners told me that he broke into this beach house where this real young thing, probably 12 or 8, I don't know, was slee'en in just shorts. When she opened her eyes, she went wide-eyed. He told her som'em like everything's c'oo, just do as I say, and I'll leave. She pushed him and they rolled on the carpet. He thought, oh shit, he'd better split. Be still, he says and holds her like…he really liked that sexy creature for a moment. She said okay, but don't hurt me, mister. My friend said he turned her over, pulled her bottoms down, and greased her with

the suntan lotion on the dresser and pushed his dick in her ass while he shoved his thumb up her little pussy. Bart

Random victimization suggests that the offender had no opportunity to assess his victim prior to raping her. That is, all he knew was that she was a female and breathing. For example:

> We breaks a lock on a railroad car full of merchandise when two guards pops us with guns in the middle of the night. My partner kicks one in the chest, I lay the other out. Both hits ground—out! I dra'em under the (railroad) car and ti'em good. But one'o'em was some cunt. Holy shit, I thought. I'm a lucky moth'a fucker today. I ripps her pants down with my knife. Marshall

In the above description, there was very little time to make a decision to rape his victim. Fact is, in most of the serial rape accounts, it appears that the offenders are acting spontaneously. But I think serial rapists have made decisions to commit the crime of rape hours, days, and/or possibly years prior to the actual attack. All that awaits the event is opportunity. Therefore, predatory rape is a conscious decision on the part of an offender. For instance Marshall added:

> Damn, my hands starts mov'en everywhere. She starts yelling and yapping like a dog, so I slap's her good. She dud'it quit. She's really nice! I pets her place (vagina). I put my thumbs over her eyes and tell her if she hurts me, I'll shoves them through her skull. I whip's out my man and feeds it to her. If she makes me come, I'll leave her be. That white trash knew her job. I was tot'en in a few minutes. We got the stuff from the (railroad) car and my partner goes down with her. I think he has (rapes) her and beats her. Marshall

Random descriptions of victim targeting included cases where a rapist found a victim while conducting other business including crimes such as robbery, criminal trespassing, and burglary. Due to the nature of random rape, lust appears to be the best predictor of serial rape under random conditions. Could some of these predators select a specific ambiance knowing they would find vulnerable victims?

Situational Targeting

Situational targeting refers to victims found in particular social environment or situation like employment. That is, in their quest for victims, the offenders sought or assessed specific situations or circumstances as opposed to specific individuals for someone to attack. Unlike random targeting where the offenders were engaged in other activities prior to discovering victims, situational rapists primary activity was the search of opportunity whereas random rape represented the opportunity. The following remarks represent 9 accounts or 15% of the sample characterizing what I refer to as situational targeting practices of the offenders.

> I worked for this outfit that was to have a big meeting in DC and I was the guy who had to make the arrangements for it. I put a ad in one of the DC papers for models using a Pittsburgh modeling agency name, and the girls came to my free suite at the hotel on a certain day and time. When I saw…Howell
>
> I travel a lot, ya know. Put a out-of-state tag on the front of my car and pull unto the driveway of houses that are being shown (For Sale). Once inside, if it's a babe show'en the place, I tell her that my wife and three kids are moving to the town. I might have to go to two or three house-openings to find the right woman. I leave, telling her I'm checking other houses out and come back just before she's ready to leave. Her defenses are

down. Look the joint over again and grab her, tossing her to the floor. Usually I want her to suck me off cause I'm not going to screw something that can give me a disease. I don't like taking to much time by undressing her either. Sometimes I tie'em up and might jack off on her if I don't want her touch'en me. Horace

Situational rapists, like the other rapists in this sample, gave the impression that they had the intention of committing rape prior to finding their victims within a particular ambience. For example:

When I was in college, I placed ads in different campus newspapers for models. If they refused sex and I really wanted them, I'd get'em high and take'em. I'd take pictures (Polaroid) in different positions. Later, if they'd say anything, I'd show'em the pictures. I liked the pictures sometimes more than sex with them. Sometimes I'd look at'em when I was hump'en one.

Sometimes, situational career rapists use the occupation of a potential victim against her to get what he wanted—sex. For example, in the following description, the offender uses her job by getting her to steel products from her employer and then intimidates her into sexual contact.

I watch'em in the stores like the mall. Especially the ones work'en the food places. Be nice to'em a few times when I buy shit. Smile. Say someth'en bout their looks. Watch'em. See if a boy friend comes. Ax'em to steel shit from work. Get'em involved. If she does it, no problem. I'll screw her and dump her. Ask? Ax her for sex instead of telling her she's going to do me?…I'm already checking out other bitches and bringing them closer. I always got a few I'm work'en with.

Again, the following narration might suggest that blaming the victim would be easy for us as we read the account of the offender. But, she is not the offender. What becomes clear is that due to her employment, she was more vulnerable to attack than other women. The following account also shows how situational rapists exploit females in a work environment.

> They should have never released me from this psychiatric hospital for criminal cats like me. I played their game and I looked straight, but they never knew my secrets. Fools! When I got on the street, the first thing I did was find a place to sleep. It was a half-way house. The social workers they sent out from the university as trainees were slower than the idiots at the hospital. I told one I had pains behind my eyes and closed them tight. I fell on the floor and rolled around like I was having a fit. She held me and I turned her on her back and throw her dress up and ripped her panties in seconds. When I shot in her, I cried. I told I didn't know what happened. If she told, they'd send me back and I didn't want to go. I told her that the other prisoners raped me and that's why I lost control. She believed me and didn't report anything. Don't ask me how she looked, but she has sexy sexy eyes that are hard to shake.

In sum, the descriptions above suggest that situational opportunities could translate into predatory rape for the offenders and that their rapes were decided upon in advance of locating a victim. Clearly opportunity is vital to criminals. That is, criminals need victims in order to attack, the intention of the attack is already present. Females who appear vulnerable are most likely to be attacked, and attack victims who learned helplessness are the victims most likely to be raped.

Confusing Statements

Sometimes, the descriptions of the predators were confusing, and I wasn't sure what victim selection category to place them in, so I chose a "confusing" category. Below are two examples of what I refer to as a confusing victim search descriptions. Perhaps you would know what to do with the 5% of these descriptions that fit into this category.

> When they say no, they don't mean it cause that's what they're best at. Gals love to screw probably more than men but they gotta be coy about it. Say'en no is a way they use to work a guy up that way they can say he owes. And I wanna tell ya about owing…buy a bitch a car, dinner, I don't care what and she says no after she get's the stuff so she can get more. They use their pussy like credit cards. Fred
>
> When I was home alone or in a break-in, I'd go through dressers looking for women's clothes like shoes, girdles, bras, panties and stuff like that. I'd wear them or sometimes just stare at'em. I'd always smell'em. When I caught girls like fish'en with drugs at the play ground, I screw'em or make'em blow me when I wear'en my girlie things. I gave her drugs and brought my friends over before she knew what was happening. They all had her. But I never let my friends see my girlie stuff. Collin

In summary, if a sexual offender perceives a female to be vulnerable or if he can manipulate her into it, he will attack. Much of an offender's perception of vulnerability has to do with the nonverbal communication of the victim.

Target Conclusions

A starting point for this discussion is that blaming the victim for the behavior of a predator is not an acceptable answer under any condition. However, much of the time, how an offender perceives his potential victim affects his decision to attack and how she responds during the attack will impact the outcome. Clearly, the information provided by the offenders lends support to serial rapists as decision makers as they themselves suggest that they are constantly scanning different social landscapes and opportunities in search of vulnerable females, regardless of how rudimentary on occasion those processes might be. Sure, they make many disgusting decisions, but all of those decisions impact the lives of other people. Fact is, predators fail more than they succeed in part because they spend more time thinking through the benefits of their attacks rather than planning them. Their attacks seem unplanned, crude, and spontaneous. They actually seem unmoved by their failures and make many attempts to succeed, despite their lazy nature. Clearly, serial rapists seek easy ways to get what they want-easy sex. The point is that females who present themselves as vulnerable and submit when attacked are at risk more than other females.

Predatory rapists rejected violence as an attack technique because their crime would take longer, and they might get hurt. Most predatory rapists are wimps. Certainly, there are some predators who enjoy violence, but most predatory rapists are fearful parasites looking for helpless and willing victims.

Looking invincible and fighting back will change the outcome of most attacks. Government statistics shows that 3 out of 4 victims of rape successfully stop their attackers. Yet, I believe that each victim needs to make her own decision about resistance since it's easy to hand advice to others when you're not threatened. I not implying that victims who have submitted were foolish since life decisions are different than arm-chair decisions. However, what juries and law enforcement personnel need to know is that predatory rape is a conscious decision made by an individual who plays a game of numbers. The more females he intimidates, the more likely he wins—not because he's smart but because he's lazy, and because others believe that they are helpless against him, no matter what they do!

CHAPTER 7

violence and serial rape

Overview of Violence

In the preceding chapter it was noted that much of the time, how a serial rapist perceives a potential victim affects his decision to attack. In this chapter it will be noted that how a victim responds during an attack, might impact the outcome of his attack. This chapter examines the extend of physical violence utilized by career rapists during their sexual attacks. While offenders offered several descriptions of murder and necrophilla, overall, violence was selective and used sparingly by chronic rapists. An implication of this discovery is that "fear entrepreneurs" sensationalize the crime of serial rape.

Controversy continues about how much violence men utilize when they are sexually assaulting strangers. A review of the popular media as presented in an earlier chapter suggests that violence is the primary motive of predatory rape, and that therefore, females who are attacked should submit or face escalated violence. Is predatory sexual assault a fulfillment of violence or sexual appetites? One answer might come from government statistics which reveal that most predatory rape victims (both attempted and completed) are not physically injured during an assault. While most jurisdictions view rape as a crime of sexual misconduct sometimes involving passion, rape is also typically reported and examined as a crime of violence. Largely predatory rape may include descriptions about vaginal and anal penetration, cunnilingus, ejaculation, and fellatio, thus sexual offenders exhibiting those actions are classified as sexually dangerous. A number of individuals claim that predatory rape includes domination, force, and coercion indicating motivational factors such as violence and the need to gain control over a victim. Yet, some describe neurological disturbances as motivators or the arousal perspective. However, recent studies show that sexual fulfillment is largely responsible for sexual attacks upon vulnerable prey by unknown predators. Caution is stressed in these studies, because indicating that motives of career rapists can be far different than other classifications of rapists such as date-rape, wife-rape, and the rape of children.

My assumptions are that predatory rapists are largely self-serving, demand instant gratification, care little about the needs of others, and as such exhibit little self-control; yet predatory rapists are in control of their facilities as they efficiently spend an enormous amount of time evaluating prey. But they are lazy and often care little about apprehended. Nonetheless, I believe that understanding offender violence can contribute to reduced victimization and improved offender rehabilitation.

Descriptions of Violence

When the descriptions of the offenders were examined together and the various levels of violence during their sexual attacks were measured, it appears that most of the respondents used violence sparingly when they assaulted their prey. Of course, there were numerous accounts described that characterized various levels of violence. Therefore, to better understand the role violence played in these attacks, I put the descriptions of the offenders into the following categories: unclear violence, nonviolence, intimidation, moderate, limited, and ultimate. Specifically, when the descriptions were placed into classifications characterizing violence (see Table 5), 18% (11) of the accounts were unclear. Thirteen percent (8) of the accounts characterized nonviolence; one criterion for this classification was that no where in these accounts was the use of force mentioned or implied before, during, and/or after the attack. Sixteen percent (10) of the rapists characterized intimidation as their only method utilized in their attacks. Specifically, threats characterized as initially being used to shock victims into submission. Twenty percent (12) of these chronic offender accounts characterized physical contact or moderate violence, but only enough to get the attention of the victim. Another 20% (12) of the accounts characterized limited violence. One criterion for this category was that these offenders used no more force than necessary to obtain their victim's submission; once submission was granted, these offenders stopped using it. But, these offenders, like all of the above stopped their attacks when threatened. Lastly, ultimate violence, aggravated force was reported in 13% (8) of the accounts before, during, and after the attacks. These individuals had no intention of stopping anything no matter what a victim did!

TABLE 4   TYPOLOGY OF VIOLENCE*   (N=61)

	PERCENTS	NUMBERS
Unclear	18%	11
Nonviolence	13%	8
Intimidation	16%	10
Moderate	20%	12
Limited	20%	12
Ultimate	13%	8
	100%	61

* The method used to arrange the categories of violence was guided by the descriptions of the offenders that characterized levels of violence as followed below

Unclear Violence Levels

Also, in 11 (10%) accounts, it was unclear how much if any violence was utilized by the rapists. For example:

> It's a numbers game. Some…believe I'd hurt'em bad if they don't suck me….If they tell me to get fucked, I find another one and eventually find the one who believes me. I ain't ask'en no babe for sex, they go'en to do it and that's the end of that tune.

In summary, of 61 cases showing various methods used by the offenders to gain victim submission, over one-half of those cases show violence as used, sparingly, for the purpose of shocking victims into sexual submission. Violence or weapons served a fundamental purpose to promote the main objective-sex.

Nonviolence

Lastly, 8 (13%) of the accounts characterize nonviolent methods of gaining victim sexual submission by the rapists. That is, these rapists say they had no physical contact other than the rape itself nor had they intimated their victims prior to their sexual success with them. For instance:

> We broke into this hospital drug store…I ducked into a room…Her body was hot…I'm feel'en her…Before anything happens, the man (hospital guard) busts me for robbery, trespassing, and rape. I didn't screw the bitch. She told the judge that I messed with her, but no way, just felt her tits. Emory
>
> Each morn'en bout 9:00 to 12:00 when I'm on the move, I check motels out cause that's when the maids are clean'em up…I'd make people for small things. One time this honey was

asleep, but I just looked till I decided to pull it (masturbated). She was asleep when I left, but I shot my wad on her. Carl

These two examples are typical of all eight descriptions offered by non-violent rapists.

Intimidation

Ten (16%) of the offenders fall into a category of violence referred to as intimidation. That is, violence was not described by the offenders themselves before or after their sexual attack. Threats characterized as initially being used to shock victims into submission are represented by the following account.

> I follow some cute babe from the parking lot at a mall. Inside, I walk up to her and ask if she owns such an' such car with such an' such tag. Maybe I describe someth'en' on the seats. I ask her bout the small animal locked in…We almost run to it…I'll say, you know what happens next. You can get hurt or it'll be over soon. She goes down on me [oral sex], and I disappear after I…Tyrone

Many of these offenders used intimidation, but only initially used it to shock their victims into sexual submission. Their main goal appears to be sexual intimacy with their victims.

Limited Violence

Twenty percent (12) of the offenders can be characterized as limited violent type rapists. One criterion for this category is that physical abuse was described as being used more than necessary to gain victim submission but that he might stop his attack when he is threatened. Also, these offenders used violence to shock a victim into submission. For instance, Yes'us explains:

> Finally, I saw this broad in the parking lot carrying a load of food with a little kid hanging on…I pushed her into the car and grabbed the kid by the throat. I slid in on top of her and said to the bitch, if you ain't a good little girl, I'll kill the kid. She mumbled something, so I slammed the shit out of her first with my free hand.

Yes'us is using more force than necessary to push his victim into sexual submission. However, he, like the other rapists who describe limited violence, can hardly take refuse in his violence as he explains further: "I told her, I want you to suck my cock. She started to but the kid won't shut up so I cracked it and she started crying too. I ran." The use of violence and submission and/or the use of a weapon both serve as a guide to put certain serial rape accounts into this category. For example:

> If they submit when I go for it, fine. When they refuse, I put a gun to their forehead. If they still say no, I smack'em with my gun. They always say yes. One time, this sweety goes no, so I said fuck you and left.

Limited violence suggests that there is a limit to the amount of violence these men would use to meet their objective. They can be stopped with their attack unlike the individuals described in the ultimate violence category. Other offenders, too, show that violence was used sparingly to get their way as in the cases of moderate violence accounts.

Moderate Violence

On the other hand, 12 (20%) of the offenders characterize physical contact but only enough to get the attention of the victim. A typical statement made by the offenders who fit this category follows:

> I called for appointments at doctor and dentists offices in another town. Their nurses would tell me when they had openings…I went to the offices when I knew the docs weren't in and three times I found a nurse'y alone. I'd made up a story about pain in my mouth, one time, and when she looked, I grabbed her hands and throw her on the floor. You know what happens next, I said to her. I had intercourse with her in the dentist's chair. Told her if she opens her mouth I'd be back, get it…opens her mouth! (He laughed. Note: he was never apprehended for these crimes).

It appears that most of the criminals who typified moderate violence rejected violence themselves and would, if confronted, stop their attack. Sexual contact was clearly their goal. Also, sometimes the inmates explain how the threat of a weapon would also be utilized to gain submission.

> If she's not watching what's happening all around her, then doesn't know how to handle herself, how to use the things around her to hurt me or get me caught. Sometimes I can go to them on the street and say shit like, okay, bitch…you know what I want and if you don't give it to me, I've got a gun in my pocket that says you're dead. I'll get in their car or they'll get in mine. If I do white stuff, she won't tell. O'Henry

Moderate offenders use a blow, a push, a slap, or threaten the use of a weapon to reach their objectives. Some of the offenders, described no physical contact with their victims other than sexual contact. Serial rapists used only enough physical contact to get the attention of the victims, but others used intimidation to obtain their goals.

Ultimate Violence

Thirteen percent (8) of the 61 heinous offenders described their forcible rape attacks with an emphasis on wicked acts of violence before, during, and after their assaults. What will be described are offenders who show that they lack limits or controls in their destruction of others. However, these descriptions demonstrate that the offender is in control of himself and in touch with reality-a reality while entirely contemptuous, yet developed and executed in a systematic process to destroy another human being in a variety of ways. In fact, in the descriptions of these ulti-mate violators, the destruction of human dignity and/or a human being is the dual goal of the offender, and sexual acts fed from the activities leading to their goals. For example:

> She was carrying a lot of packages…I open my van….my gun's look'en at her tits. From my rape case, I take out handcuffs…I took a cord from my case and tied her ankles pulling it up to her wrests. I had to check in at home so I let her in the van. Barney

One tool characterized by these offenders is anger or ultimate hatred for women which is bridged in their chronicles wailing into a storm of rage to reach their objectives. This alleged rage continues long past victim subjugation and in some cases—long past the death of their victims. Rage seemingly blinds their violence and operates as does the actual sexual assault as an alibi to exercise their destruction of another human being. If Barney pursued sexual contact, the question begging inquiry is why had he waited to complete the act? Maybe part of his systematic technique to destroy another human being is to hold his victim hostage thus breaking down her resistance and her dignity. Continuing his narration, Barney's mission materializes further in his account.

> In the middle of the night I left my warm bed and had anal sex with her (in the van). I choked her until she past out, and did it several more times. In the morning I had to take my daughters to school so I used my wife's car. When I got back, I went for a ride (in the van). Out at the city dump, I had intercourse with her and choked her again till she past out....I shaved her pussy clean and shoved my new hamper inside her. I got the handle into her rectum and moved it around a lot like a joy stick. Barney

He suggested that sexual contact is not a significant event of the abduction, but he has prioritized the systematic punishment he inflicts on his victim. He demonstrated little regard for his victim as a human being as he follows through with a seemingly proven plan of distraction. Like other violence fiends, he is able to transcend humanity—especially the humanity of his victims. His victim is the recipient whose function is to absorb his alleged rage and anger about his unsettled demands. Barney like others in this category commit the crime of rape in an effort to deal with unresolved and conflictual aspects of life. Also, rape can be an expression of power and assertion of strength and manhood. There is compelling evidence that argues "dreams" and the illusion of "a bad moth'a'fuck'a" are culturally defined and individually initiated. Maybe anger and perhaps a temper can often be explained in terms of a controlled illusion or the playing of a role. Do criminals play a self-determined role when committing criminally violent behavior? Finney's account lends some help in understanding this question:

> I tried fuck'en this cat when I was little but the fuck'en thing scratched the fuck out'a me. I grabbed that moth'a fuck'ag and

popped its fucken eyes out. I stuck my dick in its asswhole. Shit, when I shoot it was like…burning fuck'en lights in my head. Dawn…I still see'em but I ain't going to put my dick in anything without eyes…Everyday man, there's this shit in my head. Legs, asses, and foreheads of things–fuck'en things that ain't mov'en no more. Finney.

This offender's idea about reality was distorted. Necrophilia was once thought to be rare, but it is being seen more and more in the accounts of rapists. My guess is that many of the serial rapists in this category also committed the act of necrophilia, but only 2 of the participants actually described necrophilia activities. It is safe to say that Finney used a great deal of fantasy before, during, and after his encounter with his victims. In fact, my thoughts here suggest that necrophilia, having sexual relations with a corpse, can involve fantasy on the part of the rapist. Yet, let's be clear about necrophilia, it is a description, not causal in its nature.

Conclusion

Fear entrepreneurs might rule the day with giant publication distributions especially as their sensationalized accounts of violent rape tantalize the general public with misconceptions of serial rape, but this study does not support those fashionable perspectives. Maybe these fear entrepreneurs have hidden agendas that may not include victim well being. Nonetheless, based on the accounts of the respondents in this study, when I teach my daughter, Alyssa, about men: I'll tell her to fight like hell and never submit.

What also emerged from the data in this study is the fact that predators spend most of their lives in pursuit of their perversions which does not necessarily include violence. Career criminals live one life-the life of a criminal every minute or every day and that all of the events of their lives, relate to crime, one way or another. Yet, what is perplexing is that most of the respondents in this study were never apprehended for their sexual attacks and at this writing, most of them have been released from the penitentiary! The next chapter explains excessive force used during serial rape attacks.

CHAPTER 8

Excessive Force

Introduction of Excessive Force

This chapter examines the excessive force used by some predators during predatory attacks. This chapter is helpful to an understanding of serial rape in that there is a scarcity in the press discussing the excessive force used by predators from an environmental perspective. Therefore, this study will add a dimension to the media by now including a narration on the use of extreme force during the commission of the crime of rape.

After examining the characteristics described by the worst of the lot, I asked: Is human action strictly a result of an initiating factor such as attitudes, need-dispositions, or unconscious complexes? What about stimuli configurations, situational demands, or role requirements? Maybe behavior results from a process of self-interaction through which individuals experience their world from their own perspective; that is, maybe we create our own social reality in response to individual evaluation of what we see, hear, and/or feel.[36] Action has antecedent social explanations.

---

36. For a closer look see Herbert Blumer's (199?) notion of Symbolic Interactionism which suggests that human behavior is a product of an individual's interpretation of his or her social environment. Human behavior can consist of meeting a flow of situations in which individuals have to act, and that their behavior is built on the basis of what they note, assess, interpret, and what kind of projected lines of behavior they map out for themselves.

Assumptions

My assumptions are that predatory rapists are self-serving, care little about apprehension, and less about the needs of others. They exhibit little self-control during the attack itself; but, the range of self-regulated behavior which they exhibit depends on the boundaries they have placed on themselves. That is, if they reject violence as appropriate, they might utilize intimation and/or manipulation to obtain objectives of the crime of assault, sometimes, torture, and sometime murder; sometimes their interest is with necrophilla and other times with cannibalism. This chapter will examine those offenders who have placed no limits on their actions; but like other predatory offenders, they, are in control of their facilities especially since they efficiently spend an enormous amount of time seeking an opportunity to commit the crimes they have previously made a decision to commit. What will become apparent is that each serial rapist throughout each category operates in a similar style but with self-directed limits. That is, each rapist regardless of his style, continually scans his social environment for an opportunity to attack vulnerable prey. In what ways do these offenders challenge the laws of humanity?

Excessive Force Offenders

Most of the offenders in each category described behavior that characterized intimation or the use of violence sparingly, if at all, during attacks. When their victims threatened or fought back, most of the offenders stopped their attacks as quickly as they began them. But, 13% (8) of the offenders' offered descriptions of serial rape that characterized what I called supremacy rape and ultimate violence (both were discussed in the previous chapter); that is, these offenders aggravated the use of force before, during, and after victim submission. The intention of these offenders was never to stop their attack—no matter how a victim responded or the condition their victim was in including her own death! What will be described are offenders who show that they lack limits or controls in their destruction of others, and since they eroticized their criminally violent behavior, I will refer to these offenders as sadistic rapists. However, these descriptions demonstrate that the offender is in control of himself and in touch with reality-a reality while entirely inappropriate, yet developed and executed in a systematic process to destroy another human being in a variety of ways. In the descriptions of these ultimate violators, the destruction of human dignity and/or a human being is the dual goal of the sadistic offender, and sexual acts fed from the activities leading to their goals (also see Chapters 5 & 7 for other descriptions of excessive violence). For example:

Home sweet home, mom and her kid were walking down…My gun pointed at the kid…On a deserted road out of town, I stopped and told her I'd fuck. her son in the ass if she didn't have sex with me. When I was pumping away like the beautiful man I am, I told her to suck her kid. No…,, I slapped the whore. You owe me, bitch…Suck his dick or you're go'en watch that child die. Man…that got me off watch'en her do tat. When her kid came, I beat the fuck out'a both of'em and took them back to the street where I got'em from. Told that whore, you ever call the po'lice, I be back and I will fuck your kid in the ass. Then, I'll fuck your husband too. Jesse (Note: was never charged with this crime).

One tool characterized by these offenders was anger or an ultimate hatred for women which is bridged in their chronicles wailing into a storm of rage to reach their objectives. This alleged rage continues long past victim subjugation and in some cases—long past the death of their victims. Rage seemingly blinds their violence and operates as does the actual sexual assault as an alibi to exercise their destruction of another human being.

If these chronic offenders wanted sexual contact from their victims, the question begging inquiry is why do they wait to complete the act? Maybe, part of his systematic technique to destroy another human being is to hold his victim hostage thus breaking down resistance and dignity. For instance:

See I have a few drinks and go limp likes a noodle. I like to beat'em with belts and burn'em with cigarettes. Fact is, when cunts obey...I get harder. This cunt I met at a bar was in for a surprise when I took her to a party and gave her a (an) enema in front (of) my friends. I know she loved it but she screamed like a child. Most of them had (raped) her later. I got her really high on good shit and kicked her ass out of my car in the worst part of town. I came around the corner and pretended I didn't know her. Mu partner pulled her fuck'en head through the (side) window of my car. My partner held her head as I fucked her from the street with my fist. We drove off. He told me that he jerked off when he hold her head and came on her face. Far as I know, she's still there. George (Note: he implied that he was never charged with this crime).

George prioritized the systematic punishment he inflicted on his victim. He demonstrated little regard for his victim as a human being as he followed through with a seemingly proven plan of destruction. Like other violence fiends, he was able to transcend humanity—especially the humanity of his victims. These heinous offenders attacked prey in an effort to deal with their personal unresolved and conflictual aspects of their lives. Also, the attack, can be seen as an expression of power and assertion of strength and manhood especially evident in the vulgar descriptions used to characterize prey such those descriptions used by above by George.

Violence is, indeed, quicker and a short-cut to obtaining goals for many of the rapists in this study, but especially for the sadistic rapist. These violent criminals gained neither power nor sexual intimacy, although these terms may be descriptive of their behavior. Power through an illusion of sexual contact links to the ultimate goal of destruction of other human beings in a variety of ways. For example, the destruction of other human beings through the avenue of violence is in essence, the objective of these predators as characterized by the following account:

It was weird. I couldn't stop. Kind'a like in dreams. I wasn't pounding (raping) the bitch. It was like somebody else. Eddy came back (from the front seat of the car) and put it to her, too. They thought I killed her because they never heard her scream. Kicked the bitch out at (an) interstate turnoff and made sure no one saw us. But damn, some fregg'en trooper pulled us over for a tail light being out and saw the bitch's purse and blood all over me. Albert

Yet, the descriptions of the participants seem to suggest that they followed a script or played a role. For example:

We went to my room in a motel…Two girls and a guy; the guy was married to one of the bitches. They had some good dope…we was like real high, but I knew the rest of story. I grabbed one…stop, she yelled again…Her eyes just burned into me, and she tried to slide away. I slapped harder a lot of times and went for her throat. I squeezed it…She goes, why me. Fuck you, I says…Tears flooded…Her girl friend looks over while she get'en screwed and goes someth'en like, give in…I squeezed the little whore till the slut past out. Once my cock jammed this piece of trash, I let go of the neck. When the guy slept, I crawled over (to the other bed) and spread the other one (girl) out. She said someth'en like, don't….smacked her (too). I shoved it in. The guy (girl's husband) like wakes. He was like dazed. I punched the fucker-hard. He didn't move. So I came (ejaculated) on his face. Pushed his slut queen's fuck'en head in it and told her to lick it. I am the 'man' in their lives they'll never forget. I'm a bad moth'a'f…'a, bad! Before I go, I pulled the fuck'en nipple

of the other bitch and shoved a pin through it. Took their fuck-
'en drugs and money and split. Nick

Nick's description of his activities resembled other descriptions which
characterized a playing of a role. Do sadistic rapists play a self-determined
role when committing corrupt acts? Ted's account lends some help in
understanding this question:

> I got started messing women's bodies up when I was young.
> I'd cut pictures of women, along their body lines, from the Sears
> catalog. Then I'd cut body parts from Playboy or one of those.
> When I wanted to undress the pure women in Sears, I'd use the
> nude parts from Playboy or Hustler so I could see her face but
> her body was naked. Sometimes I'd cut men's dicks out and
> add'em to the pictures. I'd see the face of the pure women, the
> body from Playboy and a man's dick sticking out from her. I
> could take other women, undress her and play with the cut-outs
> so that it would look like a woman with a man's thing, screw'en
> another woman. When I was older, I'd make appointments with
> women lawyers and shrinks. If they looked like any of the
> women I created, I'd think about it when I made myself come. A
> couple of times, I played real stupid and non-threatening. I
> made my move and pulled out my gun forcing this pure lawyer
> bitch to the floor. Shit, just telling you about it is getting me up
> (erect)! I dressed an undressed her in her office. Ted

Ted created a sense of social reality that relates to his version of his past
experiences. In the rest of his narrative, he seems to fulfill his role objectives complete with obligations and expectations. For instance:

> I pulled out some of my pictures that were taped together and
> laid them on her face. I masturbated and came on her being

careful not to hit my pictures. She wasn't so pure when I got done with her. I never got caught because I kept moving around. One time though I cut her up and wanted to put her body parts onto another women, but I had to stop because I really didn't want to hurt her. I hated myself for being a coward so I shot her and moved to another town...

Action that appears to be fueled by anger could be explained in terms of the assumptions about role obligations guided by trial and error experiences and expectations. We see that Ted has created an illusion about the expectations of both his real victim and his imagined victim. The accounts of these offenders offer what appears to be compelling testimony that supports a perspective of an illusion of what "a bad moth'a'fuc'a" is to these offenders. Clearly their idea is culturally defined and individually initiated. These offenders think that they are playing a role of sorts during their concert during their attacks. Perhaps by knowing the outcomes of their behavior, a small window if you will, can help us see that these offenders are acting from a script they wrote. For example, Ted revealed:

Yea, sure...I screwed her good. Her blood was all over me, the pig, so I slapped her...know what? She couldn't hit me back!...maybe, there were others like her....I told yea, doc, yea. I had sex with her when she was dead not because I'm weird, but because I could make her face look like my pictures. I set her face up with a smile or whatever and that's the way she'd look....I'd cut eyes of my girls and put them over her closed eyes that way she watched me and smiled the whole time. Got it? Ted

When Ted performed the role of an "attacker," he perceived the appropriate behavior for that role or what can be called a self-fulfilling prophecy. He acted out the obligations and expectations of an attacker and/or the obligations of "a bad moth'a'fuc'a." When his victim does not meet the perceived obligations and expectations of her role as the victim, he interjects his ideals upon her.

Necrophilla, too, is an issue that must be examined. My guess is that the ultimate violence rapists also committed necrophilla, but only 2 of the participants actually described necrophilla activities. Yet, let's be clear about necrophilla; it's a description, not a causal factor to heinous acts. Clearly, finding satisfaction by degrading, beating, and sometimes killing a victim, then engaging in sexual contact with that victim takes patience, skill, and motivation, but above all, it takes playing a role of an offender who has eroticized these activities. In that way, the offender has transcended humanity and sees himself as something more than a human being. For example, "Me," revealed Smitty, "bit'en a piece of meat off'a dead cunt, I've just blew my wad (ejaculation) in, shows that I'm good and bad—the worst nightmare she's ever come across." The accounts of these foul rapists were consistent with Ted Bundy and Edward Gein in that both offenders thought they were inherently evil in themselves.[37]

conclusion

Criminally violent offenders, who use excessive force, often commit the crimes of murder, rape, and necrophilla with the same victim. They create their own illusion of reality; often times the meaning, relevance, and goals of these illusions are only known by an individual offender. These illusions are usually guided by the experiences of an offender through a process of trial and error and personal assessment–an assessment or interpretation of

---

37. See Ann Rule (1980) for accounts on Ted Bundy and Judge Robert H. Gollmar (1981) for accounts on Edward Gein.

the world furthered by role expectations and obligations. To learn the extend of an offender's criminal history might be to discover his attitudes about the expectations and obligations of the role he played especially when attacked others. That is, if he thinks he is god or the devil then perhaps, it might lead to a self-fulfilling prophecy of life or death of others which are both within his perceived province.

Simply explaining supremacy or control and power via violence, the popular view as found in magazines, newspapers, and Hollywood as a causal model, leaves many questions. Good social science research should make obvious that which is obvious, rather than offering popular explanations.[38] One thought here is that an individual who destroys other human beings sees himself as an individual above the law of both man and nature or God—he sees himself as playing the role of evil, it could be argued from the descriptions of the offenders. Therefore, to re-examine a naturalistic analysis in terms of supernaturalistic dimensions might provide one answer. This is not an invitation to examine demonic or supernatural beliefs of ancient civilizations. Let's think above the culturally confines of a purely naturalistic view that often becomes preoccupied with testable explanations of things in this world which forgets to consider their moral, spiritual, or cosmic dimensions of crime. The role of evil or demonic possession with all its inhuman characteristics, could be believable when trying to understand how criminals can easily surpass the very nature of being human by performing some of the activities as those revealed in this study. But there is a major deficit in criminal research or investigation by which to

---

38. For indepth reading on this thought see writers like Peter Berger. Then, too, had not history taught us that the ideas of some individuals like those of Socrates, Jesus, Mohammed, Galileo, Marx, and Dr. Martin Luther King, Jr. were considered radical and insane by others in their day. Clearly, this writer possesses no similarity or significance as compared to those individuals, but, I ask: why would certain individuals in our society ultize so much systematic force to destroy another human being?

judge the evils of the modern criminal.[39] Therefore, I might argue that many sophisticated theories are probably in the dark ages about violence, partly due to the conservative nature of some writers and the difficulty of publishing less than traditional ideas. A few writers have examined the role of evil as explanations for various crimes.[40] Yet, few writers specifically talk about evil and serial rape. In fact, there appears to be a "scared void" in place in the both research and in the crime lab about evil and obeying the role of evil. Stanford Lyman (19??, p.1) continues this thought:

> Evil is a term that is rarely found in a modern sociology text…To the extent that sociological thought embraces the study of evil today, it does so under the embarrassing, neutered morality of deviance. Adopting for the most part an uncritical stance toward the normative structure of any given society, the…sociologist of deviance takes his cue from whatever the forces of law and restriction define as evil. Hence, the concerns of the vocal and powerful elements of a society become the resources for a sociological investigation of evil.

Serial rapists who engage in criminally violent behavior as described by sadistic rapists are men moved by acceptance of a force that I will refer to as evil. My definition of evil includes a range of behavior that criminally attacks human dignity to destruction of a human life. Whether the evil the participants possess originated outside of themselves or those individuals created it—is insignificant to the results of their behavior. More than likely, these individuals have produced their own sense of corruption in

---

39. For more information on this perspective see Stanford Lyman (19??).
40. See Fred E. Katz (19??).

that they have taken the role of an individual they perceive as the devil, as themselves. My subjects perceived themselves as evil and therefore, acted according to their perception of the role. As suggested by W.I. Thomas, if individuals "define situations as real, they are real in their consequences."

By showing how violent and corrupt they can be, the more they perceived that they are the evil one....the one who the Judaic-Christian Bible condemns! Doing corrupt acts makes them unique and special, they surprise, as their battle of dominance is with God's children. Therefore, ugly sadistic rape is their way "of making a mark upon God's world." It's their way of telling others that they are significant in this world. In a sense, acting evil can be the opposite of acting divine. For example, necrophilla involves holding a god-like power (the opposite of evil) over an individual. The finality of death, is not the last decision made by a god of darkness. Gods have many decisions to make and perhaps their decisions, or so these offenders implied, are part of what helps this offender physically and psychologically meet their objectives.

Recall what Charles Manson, Ted Bundy, and Pe Wee Gaskins have told us about their relationship with evil. In Pe Wee's terms, "I am god-the god of death." He and others believe it to be true! I believe that they have told themselves hard enough and long enough and have demonstrated to themselves and others how bad and corrupt they are—now, they believe it. In my own experience, many violent offenders tend to describe themselves as "I'm bad, mannn, real bad!" What has become clear in these pages is that these men have accepted an evil role, and will do everything to prove it.

Is it possible that ordinary people can become extraordinary evil in their behavior? In a sense, some of my recent research suggests that nonviolent offenders can become violent offenders due to a process of prisonisation, however, that research related to incarcerated offenders. But, Fred Katz suggests that noncriminals or ordinary people can engage in evil too. He claims that only a tiny proportion of this century's massive killings are attributable to the actions of those people we call criminals, or crazy people, or socially alienated people, or even, people we identify as evil people.

The vast majority of killings were actually carried out by plain folks in the population—ordinary people like you and me. Certainly the Hitlers and Stalins of our world produced plans for evil that boggle the imagination. But who transformed these plans into action? To Hitler and his cause they donated their energies, their skill, and their very lives, often doing so with joyful abandon.

I believe that a better understanding of how ordinary behavior is changed, would help it continue unhampered. Yet, some individuals who read these pages might reject the realities of evil-doers much as others had throughout the history of every civilization. That is, a society can either honestly confront the realities of myths or face decline. The realities of sadistic rapists who utilize excessive force and commit the crime of murder during a serial rape attack have been explored and two points must be made about them: (1) rehabilitation is futile; and (2) only their total destruction will stop them. However, it should be noted that most serial rapists use force sparingly if at all. Further research is called for on the detection of serial rapists.

For thought, many violent offenders demonstrate criminally violent characteristics when they are four or five years old, some writers like Stanton Samenow inform us. It would seem logical therefore to spend our enormous law and order expenditures on our children rather than on our offenders. That is, government statistics report that the United States spends far more money on cops and corrections than teachers, schools, and family well-being. Certainly, if American society redirects its resources on its young, then adults can bass in the sun of safety without the purchase of a weapon and the necessary training to use those weapons effectively.

APPENDIX 1

University Student Evaluation

We carefully studied each statement for many, long months. Completing my evaluation, I felt I had been objective in my conclusions, but perhaps because of the way I felt, I'm probably biased. Nonetheless, as fate had it, my family and I moved from Buffalo, New York to Charlotte, North Carolina after my contract expired at Attica Penitentiary in the fall of 1993. I would be in front of 55 new traditional college students who had no idea who this criminologist was or what ideas I had about predatory rapists. It was a perfect opportunity. Although, my class was an advanced class in Sociological Deviance, I handed my new students 61 statements describing serial rape activities on the second class day. I asked them to evaluate the statements and to create a motive and target typology—a set of categories in which to place each rapist's narrative. They had three weeks to make their evaluation, and during those three weeks, the subject of predators was not discussed. I also advised them that we could not talk about motivation or causal effects of crime in that class until their work was completed. That is, the students knew that there were no right or wrong answers and all they had to do using those 61 statements was to answer the following questions:

1. When the responses of the inmates are pooled, the most frequently self-reported objective promoting predatory rape was:
2. When the responses of the inmates are pooled, the most frequently self-reported method of selecting their victims was:
3. When the responses of the inmates are pooled, create a typology (categorize) the violence descriptions presented by the offenders used during their attacks?

Much of their thoughts were congruent with the ideas of the inmates-interviewers who created similar typologies, and my own thoughts. Therefore, I knew I was on the right track. Most of us, of course, have our own thoughts about predators, and most of those thoughts have to do with how much punishment criminals deserve. Nonetheless, many of the offenders in this study have been released as of this writing.

APPENDIX 2

Method and Sample

I trained 13 incarcerated violent offenders enrolled in a university course entitled Sociology of Crime at a maximum custody prison as student-interviewers. The students attended several lectures and participated in many classroom discussions on researcher bias and interviewing techniques over a fifteen week period. Some of the things they learned included ideas such as: subjects tell interviewers what they think the interviewers want to hear whether the research is conducted in prison or a shopping mall. We had practice sessions, too, which needless to say, were memorable. The inmate-interviewers were told not to tell other inmates what they were studying, but more importantly, I never told the inmate-interviewers the information I sought. Besides, it would be many months after gathering all of the data and carefully studying it that I would know what it all meant. When I learned many of the things I now know, I reviewed those findings with inmate students at Attica in New York where I also I taught and facilitated class style encounter sessions with rapists and murderers.

Student-Interviewers

Each student-interviewer recruited 5 volunteers from his cellblock to discuss predatory crimes prior to incarceration. These discussions were designed to keep the subjects and interviewers comfortable as they unrevealed predatory accounts. Typical interviews lasted over an hour and were conducted in various locations throughout the prison. Neither the researchers nor the subjects received any monetary gain for their participation; however, the student-interviewers received 3 university credit hours for completion of the course.

I also conducted 20 interviews with inmates and had the help of correctional officers in locating volunteers who knew something about predatory crime. To insure confidentiality, those interviews were conducted in a prison classroom. Although, I never knew any of the names of the inmates I interviewed, my reputation as a prison teacher and group facilitator holding many inmate confidences apparently helped the interview process as many of the participants seemed uninhibited after several minutes of general discussion. I keyed their statements into a computer, if they agreed, and all but 4 had, during the interview. My data and the data of the student-interviewers were similar. A total of 85 inmates were interviewed in the spring of 1992. Of the 85 total interviews-only 61 were considered reliable.

One student-interviewer allegedly interviewed 5 inmates but his interviews were challenged by his peers; 3 inmates were interviewed twice; 2 informants admitted to only male rape; 1 inmate raped only children, 8 informants had not admitted to predatory rape, and 5 cases were so confusing or poorly written by student-interviewers that I pitched them out. Therefore, subjects who served as participants included individual male prisoners incarcerated in a high custody facility who admitted to committing predatory rape before confinement. I have only 265 detailed accounts of serial rape as offered by the sample since many of them could not remember all of their experiences, but kept count and did present brief descriptions, without detail of their crimes.

Criminal Validity

To enhance validity of this study, I collected data through inmate-interviewers, conducted 20 interviews myself for purposes of validity, and discussed all the findings with other offenders and other prison professionals in other high custody prisons. Most indicated that the accounts of the participants as accumulated by the inmate-interviewers and myself appeared realistic, and they were able to relate the findings to their experiences with other apprehended predators they had known.

APPENDIX 3

Type of Questions

Some of the questions asked using A. Nicholas Groth's "Protocol for the Clinical Assessment of the Offender's Sexual Behaviors" as a guide used question prefixes like "if rape happened." Topics included were:

1. Premeditation

To what extend did you plan the offense? Did you set in search of a victim with a deliberate intent to commit sexual assault? Did the idea suddenly come to mind when an opportunity presented itself? In terms of importance before a rapist attacks a female he doesn't know, what should he do first: Rank order the following if 1 is the first thing and 6 the last or just say you don't know: be sure she's alone, old enough, going to like it, drunk/stoned, not a fighter, pretty.

2. Victim Selection

What were the descriptive characteristics (age, race, sex, situation, physical characteristics) of the victim, and what part did each play in the your selection? Was there a relationship with the victim prior to the incident? What was it about the physical characteristics of the victim that made her the victim? Could you have had sex with anyone else at the time? Can you describe the victim? Do you recall what she looked like?

3. Style of Attack

How did you gain control over your victim? Did you use description and entrapment, threat or intimidation, physical force or violence, or some combination of those techniques? How did you gain sexual access to your victim? Did you render your victim helpless through drugs or alcohol? Did you make promises to the victim that you couldn't keep?

4. Accompanying Fantasies

What were you fantasizing during the aback? Was the victim in your fantasies identifiable? Did the attack go as you dreamt it? When did these fantasies first begin? Often did they repeat themselves?

5. Role of Aggression

How seriously did you want to hurt your victim? Under what conditions would you resort to physical force during the rape? How excising was the real force that you used? Did it turn you on?

6. Sexual Behavior

What was going on sexually during the rape (kissing, fondling, masturbating, breast sucking, digital penetration, vaginal intercourse, oral intercourse, or anal contract, etc.) Did you tie the victim? Did you ask the victim to act out any role or get into various sexual positions? Did you get off? Did she phase you? Were you frustrated or disappointed after the rape? How long did it last? How did you think she felt during and after the offense?

7. Contributing Factors

What triggered the rape? Responsibility: are you admitting to the rape?

8. Recidivism

Ain't sa'en you did nothing, but in your dreams about how many times might you of raped a girl you didn't know?

9. Deterrence

What could the victim do to stop rape from happening.

10. Martial Relations

When you were a free man, how was your sex at home?

APPENDIX 4

Who Were The Offenders In This Study?

According to the responses of the offenders, the average respondent was 32 years old (see Table 4). Fifty-six percent (34) of the participants were black, 41% (25) white, and 3% (2) Hispanic whose average education was 8th grade, prior to this conviction. Thirty-one percent (19) were married, 69% (42) were single and/or divorced, and 66% (40) reported having a regular sex life prior to incarceration. Sixty-three percent (38) of the respondents reported that they held a menial job (such as house care maintenance and auto service station workers), 10% (6) reported a white collar job (such as CPA and high school teacher), and 37% (17) reported being unemployed prior to incarceration. Yet, 70% (43) of both the employed and the unemployed reported earning most of their spending money from an illegal source such as hustling, theft, and drug trafficking. The typical respondent reported being arrested 3.4 times and he had served an average of 84 months.

Sixty-five percent (40) of the participants had been convicted of a crime of violence. What the participants reported and what the records of the participants showed about their convictions were similar That is, 5% (3) were convicted of homicide (murder and manslaughter), 5% (3) armed robbery, 28% (17) of aggravated assault, and 28% (17) of sexual assault. And, 35% (21) were convicted of a crime of nonviolence. That is, 18% (11) were convicted of a parole violation 18% (11), 10% (6) larceny, and 7% (4) drug/alcohol related crimes.

Table 4   Average Characteristics of Offenders   (N=61)

CHARACTERISTICS	AVERAGE/PERCENT	Range/numbers
Age	32	18-52
Race		
Black	56%	34
White	41%	25
Hispanic	3%	2
Education	8	2-17
Married	31%	19
Single/Divorced	69%	42
Regular Sex Life	66%	40
Menial Jobs	62%	38
White Collar Jobs	10%	6
Unemployed	27%	17
Illegal Incomes	43%	26
Arrests	3.4	1-14
Months Served	84	1-135
Convictions		
Homicide	5%	3
Armed Robbery	5%	3
Aggravated Assault	28%	17
Sexual Assault	28%	17
Parole Violation	18%	11
Larceny	10%	6
Drug/Alcohol	7%	4

Data Collection

Data collection and analysis proceeded simultaneously in keeping with Barney Glasser and Anselm Strauss' perspectives of "grounded theory." Both process and products of research were shaped from the statements made by the offenders. Fresh theoretical interpretation was sought from offender statements and checking inmate records and a questionnaire helped gather information about race, age, arrest rates, and so on. There were 265 detailed accounts of serial rape offered by the sample since many of them could not remember all of their experiences, but kept count and did present brief descriptions, without detail of their crimes. When I reviewed the account-sets (265 accounts in 61 sets) of valid descriptions, I chose one typical description that best characterized each set (participant). Once completed, the typical descriptions were compared, analyzed, and similar descriptions were put into a typology of rape. Therefore, I examined 61 descriptions that typified motives, target selection, and violence used reports of each participant; using a number of tests including ideas shared by students, colleagues, and correctional personnel especially social services those descriptions produced eight mutually exclusive categories (including an unclear category) presenting a motive typology; similar tests were used to develop a target selection typology comprised of four mutually exclusive categories, and a violence used typology comprised of six mutually exclusive categories. When these typologies were compared with academic and mainstream literature, distinctive differences emerged.

Interviews

The average interview lasted approximately fifty minutes with a range from fifteen minuets to a two hours. Concerns about an inmate's age, education, and other demographic questions were asked on a questionnaire given each inmate prior to his interview. Statements about serial rape and other crimes were made to inmate-interviewers and to myself at a maximum custody prison. The inmate-interviewers wrote the statements that applied to serial rape and other crime as they spoke with the offenders they interviewed. When I interviewed 20 offenders, I first tried to tape-record their conversations, but the offenders were reluctant to speak about their affairs. Yet, they allowed me to enter their statements into a computer, providing there were other statements on the screen.

Therefore, using each category as a guideline, my best interpretation about the experiences of the predatory rapists regarding motives, violence

Limitations of This Study

However, there are limits on my work that must be clear before generalizing the conclusions of this paper. For example, I examined only incarcerated offenders who were predominantly from the lower socioeconomic class, thus, I believe that the results are generalizable only to those individuals with similar characteristics. Also, I measured specifically serial rape explanations and argue that other types of rape, such as date rape, may have significantly different characteristics than serial rape. And lastly, my unique orientation as a researcher, teacher, and adviser of high risk felons and enforcement agencies and officers, might differently effect my judgements about offenders than other writers.

APPENDIX 5

Race of Victims

If we believe the self-reported data of the offenders, all of the offenders said that they had raped white females more often than females from other races. Also, 75% (26) of the black rapists and 3% (2) of the Hispanic respondents described only white victims in all of their predatory rape accounts.

The fact that majority of black and Hispanic offenders were allegedly interracial rapists might call to question the punch of this study as this data are conflicting from virtually all scientific study results.[41] One reason for this inconsistency relating to interracial rapes could be that offenders tend to be incarcerated more often depending upon the race of their victims as opposed to the seriousness of their criminal acts. Thus, black on black crime may be different from black on black conviction rates. What is also known about rape in general, depending upon whose estimates you want to believe, is that fewer black women report rape than white women. Female rape victims in victimization reports confirm interracial activity, but, if some women have different perceptions about how others view the race of their attacker, some women might lie about it. Other reasons could be that the subjects were lying about their victims in order to enhance their reputations with inmate-interviewees as white women victims may be perceived as more valuable prey, per say, than black victims. Also, all of the white offenders said that they had raped only white victims. Of course, all of the above could be true if we lived in an all white world but it sounds doubtful. What might help, however, with the idea that white women are targeted more often than black women is the idea tht black women tend not to be as vulnerable as white women. That is, black women might not as a group accept as often the idea of a learned helplessness as often as white women making black women as a group less desirable as a target.

Lastly, the participants revealed few family ties as adults and perceived themselves as loners during childhood. Only 7% of the subjects reported that they were first-time violent offenders. It appears that most of the participants represent the habitual prisoner.

CHAPTER 9

Inside the Head of a Rapist

To better understand the strategies embraced by chronic sexual offenders, their typical lifestyle experiences beg attention. What follows is a brief narration or typical life profile of a sexual offender based on similarities in the accounts of offender as they experienced youth, manhood, and prison. This composite produces a window into the compelling dynamics that help shape the faulty decision making processes of a sexual offender. His name is Darin, and he will be out of prison by the time you read these pages. He served four years and two months for assault and theft despite all of the crimes he had visited on women and children. Darin is a drip of man, tipping the scales at one hundred and thirty pounds; he stands close to five nine; he's an individual who can smile endlessly about anything including the plague. When he stands still, some people might guess his age at 32, but when he talks he seems younger. He is an intensive listener with a steady smile and round eyes that lock on yours almost as if he were a priest. When he talks, his voice chimes with a freshness that gives the impression he is a bright college graduate emerging himself in the nuances of a new career, even when he's describing his crimes. Descriptions such as handsome, charming, and sensitive are used by police officers who arrested him, correctional officers who guard him, and psychologists who evaluated him. His victims called him manipulative and dangerous. He is a predator who can never be cured, but should some unsuspecting wizard help in the process, only a stone-cold god could forgive him. Judge for yourself!

His parents met at high school, graduated a year apart from each other, married before they were twenty, and now live several blocks from their early childhood homes. Darin has a younger brother and sister. His parents often were away from home and when he was younger, his aging grand-mother and aunt watched over them. Nonetheless, Darin, a very active child, was alone most of the time since his grandmother and aunt favored his passive brother and sister. When his parents were home, they bitterly quarreled and threw things at each other often leaving Darin to a spot in a cluttered closet. His brother and sister always took refuse with his aunt.

Before first grade Darin experienced masturbation; it brought him immediate relief and he described feelings of serenity. A lack of attention gave him the opportunities to explore his sexuality, fantasies, and feelings. As Darin grew, he looked inward for comfort, withdrawing from others and outside activities, as most proved tedious. The outside world and all of its events were a bitter disappointment prolonging his stress and hard-ships. The more he withdrew, the more he overcame his feelings of alien-ation and frustration, and the more he lied about his behavior, his whereabouts, and his desires.

At school, since academics came easy to him he focused on human behavior through observation of others while most students focused on skills through teachers, workbooks, and rules. For instance, Darin studied the teacher and students while everyone else followed a reader in their lit-erature book. He also learned by "doing and taking chances." For exam-ple, when he took the coat of another student, he wore it to go home, but was caught before leaving school. He often said shocking things to stu-dents to watch their reactions. Another way he learned about behavior was by playing the class clown; being funny allowed him access to every per-sonality in the class. When other boys challenged him to a fight, Darin made them his allies with the biting rational of a combat commander. Fighting was not one of Darin's strengths.

At home when he masturbated, he might try to recall the response of a girl at school to his earlier antics; this activity was his way of intimacy without dealing with them. At school the next day, he stared at the girl while to recall his ejaculation, but never could. It sounded as though he wanted to be satisfied without exhausting much effort.

When Darin was in sixth grade, he often babysat Tammy, a 4 year old girl who lived next door, while her mother went on errands. Tammy's daddy lived elsewhere. He wondered how much Tammy would like to bite his penis and how large her eyes would grow when he "shoot" (ejaculated) in her month. Each time he babysat, he got braver. He decided that she liked being touched everywhere especially her back. He smoothed his index finger on the outside of her vagina and tried to push his fingers in her; he remembered stopping because he saw droplets of blood coming from her little body. He studied each careening droplet with intensity, he recalled, and now tried to convince me that he felt sorry for the pain Tammy experienced. Several times he ejaculated on her bare buttock as he pretended to be spank her. A few times he ejaculated on her face. He recalled one time wiping her face quickly as he heard her mother's vehicle enter their garage. He tickled Tammy forcing wide smile as her mother walked into the cozy front room. Tammy's mother kissed her cheek, the very cheek he had wiped his sperm from. When asked how he felt about that experience, a huge smiled crowded his face and he continued to discuss the experience with the urgency of a used car salesman. Darin said that he wondered how Tammy and her mother would look having sex together. Years later, when Darin attacked a woman and her young son, he remembered the "cheek experience;" he said that he became so excited by its memory that he cohered the woman into oral sex on her son; then raped her and maculated the boy.

Darin often engaged in house break-ins, shoplifting, and school vandalism alone. He liked the idea that he could outsmart adults by committing crimes, although he never referred to them as crimes—just games. Every so often he tried different drugs including uppers and downers but didn't like the effect they had on him; to outwit others and to avoid apprehension, he had to be in control of himself. However, he often lost control of himself when he had intercourse and most of the time, it was "my duty to come deep inside her body," Darin proclaimed. The practice of forced intercourse, to the day of the interview, was his obsession and salvation.

Even when he might masturbate, he rammed his penis in the vagina of his victim when he ejaculated, "to get her fluids on me. That made me harder in the days ahead." No matter how old he was, weeks after a forced sexual encounter with a female, he had little difficulty in an erection. But several weeks after the attack, becoming erect would happen only as he attacked another female. Prison is an excellent laboratory! Darin was not able to have forced sex with females, and consequently was rarely erect although he had sexual relations with other inmates. He described experiences that seemed to relate to a drug addict instead of a sexual offender. Might there be a correlation between forced intercourse and addiction, I thought?

When he was in ninth grade, he and Tammy played many games together such as baker and doctor. He waited for an opportunity to teach her how to make him have an ejaculation using her hands. He tried many ways during the games and finally succeeded. He convinced Tammy that she was a bad girl, and he would tell her mother. As expected, she cried and cried until he promised he wouldn't tell! "Let's keep our secret," he said. Molesting the child was a simple task after that–no more games. Next, he taught her how to make him have an ejaculation using her month, but he usually had to masturbate and feed his penis into her mouth.

At 16, he pretended to be asleep on Tammy's mother couch when he heard her arrive at home after a date. She was in the washroom on the toilet when attacked her. He was unsuccessful. He cried, telling her that he thought of her, as his mother, and that he didn't know why he behaved the way he had. She forgave him. Weeks later, he broke into her home, filled the bathtub with water, waited for her to come home from work, and emerged himself in the water pretending to commit suicide. Her motherly hands saved him from his dome, and he can still talk about the kindness of her touch. A few times when he had concentrated on her rescue, he pricked his scrotum with a sewing pin when he masturbated at home.

Several months later, he crawled through a window and attacked her as she slept. The police were called. Darin cried and wailed in pain. He said that the woman often forced him into having oral sex and that this time he refused. After an investigation, they charged her with felony rape. Darin refused to testify, and the charges against her were dropped.

He eventually moved from his childhood home, but returned to rape her two more times. The third time, as she slept he tied a noose around her neck. He dragged her from bed to the floor, and choked her until she performed oral sex while Tammy watched until he locked her in the closet; he tied Tammy's mother to the bed, shoved some amphetamines down her throat, pushed a few straight-pins thorough her nipples, and sexually assaulted her with sex toys; he said he wanted to show her that he was an adult and not a child. He also said that he was angry that she had betrayed him by calling the police on him in the past. Now, he wanted to call the police and this time, "I will testify," he sniveled repeatedly in her ear! As his last act, he brought Tammy back into the bedroom and pulled her pajamas from her. He put the large sex toy close to her vagina, "If you report me, I'll be back," said he. He stole several items from her home and threw them in the river on his way to his uptown apartment.

As a student at a local community college, Darin took an internship at a summer children's camp. He had sexually attacked a boy and a girl; he succeeded with the boy but could not have an ejaculation although he was erect. Darin told his victim that he, the boy, was a homosexual and had brought the attack upon himself by attacking Drain with "a secret fag eye beam." Darin said that he wouldn't tell the others about the incident if the boy didn't use his bean on others and if he remained in his room pretending to be sick. Darin visited him several times, but did not have sex with him. He tightly held the boy and stroked his hair, even though he believed that the boy enjoyed their earlier sexual encounter.

Largely, Darin maintained temporary friendships and avoided females who lacked an aggressive nature. He exaggerated friendships and relationships with aggressive girls in order to manipulate them to be his sexual partner. What he liked about aggressive girls was that they were strong willed and could manipulate his penis as forcefully as he had, but some of those females wanted to be satisfied too. He wasn't interested in mutual satisfaction. Since he didn't want or know how to behave in an ongoing relationship, most of those relationships ended soon after they began. To Darin, people who understood him were treats, but acquaintances were impressed with his charm. He hated being charming. Several times Darin tried to kill himself but never succeeded. Since he laughed while he explained each of those occurrences, I took that to mean that he could have used those events to manipulate others.

Darin had a brief sexual affair with one of his male instructors at the community college. Darin was easily leered into the relationship but soon dominated it; he took the instructor's credit cards and used his car for a month. Darin told the man that he would tell everyone about their relationship if he reported him. As the opportunities presented themselves, Darin had sexual relations with other homosexuals he had met through his teacher. Shortly thereafter, the instructor quit his job and moved to away, or so Darin explained. As his mother and others inquired as to Darin's whereabouts, he lied and kept his life a secret from everyone including the police when they investigated the disappearance of the college instructor.

Sex in itself was boring, but rape got him what he wanted–forced sexual intercourse. He believed that he had given his victims what they wanted, too. In answer to the question about committing predatory rape, he said:

"It's difficult to describe something invisible stirring inside your belly reaching into the muscle-lining of your throat demanding I do something! Deciding, all right tonight, I'll cruise and find some morsel to feed you. Leave me be. Festival (his term for sexual attacks) is near."

Attacking a female was the only way of feeling good and eventually he decided that his female victims felt good about his attack too since they submitted easily to his demands. In his mid-twenties, he performed well at work, but he could never get sexual attacks out of his head or the feeling from the huge icy brush that scratched his penis as he looked around the office. "Maybe a quickie at lunch?"

He married a woman he met at work. She worked in the mailroom. He was a rising executive. People often asked Darin why he married an older and heavier woman than himself. He told them that "love is greater than fat!" The first time they dated, she got drunk—he raped her. Their sexual relationships were usually on a roller coaster depending on how Darin felt; he practiced some of his attack holds on her to see which ones worked and which ones didn't.

Every so often, he drove or flew to different destinations to attack females. Sometimes he attacked vulnerable females and sometimes he tried to manipulate others into vulnerable situations, but mostly he failed. Most of his victims worked in offices in small strip malls and the least of his victims were in motels and restaurants. He succeeded every few months and was almost apprehended once. The way he described his feelings was, "Everything that flows through my mind, every imagine swallowed by my brain, every smell, are focused on festival. I must smell the fright of a woman when she knows she's going to give in because that's what god made her for—and I must taste her sweat when I finish her off because she worked so hard to please me. They love it doc; they really love being forced. But, I'm dying a thousand deaths in here (prison) because I need…a girl, any girl to love." The last time Darin held his young daughter during a prison visit, he wondered how much she wanted to put her lips around his penis and how large her eyes would get when he would shoot inside her mouth. He loved her smell and couldn't get her scent out of mind for several months.

CHAPTER 10

Serial Rape Conclusion

Popular writers suggest control, power, and violence are the primary objectives of predatory rapists. Those writers preach that women should never resist predators; they advocate that a victim can expect escalated violence and sometimes death should they resist because of those objectives. But, these ideas are largely unsupported by serial rapists!

One reason for this serious difference of opinion is that fear entrepreneurs sensationalize predatory rape and others "politicize" it. In fact, government statistics reveal that most serial rape victims are never injured during the commission of this horrible crime. Possibly, popular writers and their politically correct partners created an information rape cartel centered in a groupthink process which they can not reject at this time for fear of looking ill advised. They are the writers who suggest that all men are potential rapists! After the average god-fearing male reads the accounts of predators and thinks he's anything like the men in this study, then it might be safe to say that all women are potential whores, and we know that isn't true either!

Is human conduct, such as the conduct of a serial rapist, a result of an initiating set of diabolical factors such as majestic cultural objectives, mysterious unconscious complexes energized by DNA deposits, and/or subliminal stimuli configurations? Frankly, one practical way to understand behavior is that it largely results from a continual process of self-interaction through individual interpretation of an environment; we decide on a response that best brings us closer to our goal (for the moment), and do it—limited by our physical capabilities, experiences, and expertise.

Behavior changes depending on how we see a situation or an interaction linked to our goals.

One incident such as serial rape should never be viewed as an isolated event should we wish to understand and hopefully control predators. Predatory rape is a series of ongoing conscious lifestyle decisions made by a predator as he lives his life. A psychological dependence and possibly, a physiological dependence to engage in a forced sexual encounter with a female are the sparks that guide his decision moving toward sexual attacks. With that much heat, he has little chose in the matter should he wish to extinguish the flames in his head. First, the rapist must find a victim, so he's looking for opportunity. Power, control, and violence might be merely the interpretations of how popular writers view most serial rapists; yet, most of their attacks can be stopped when the victim doesn't think or act like a victim.

Most predatory rapists understood their feelings, their experiences, and the consequences of their criminal behavior. Simply put, like most human conduct, rapists said that there were no giant mysteries surrounding their sexual attacks. Tragically, most of them would have stopped what they were doing if they chose or if their victims fought back. For one, if a female fought her attacker she would have felt better regardless of the outcome of the attack. For a very few of the offenders, only their own destruction would have stopped them. Actually, I had expected many more of these offenders to be in this last category, but what I learned about serial rape seems to be different than what many writers have led us to believe. What seems to be in question, therefore, is how much are we willing to learn from the experts-by-experience?

Specifically, the primary mission of most serial rapists is to have immediate sexual contact with a female–any female. Some rapists say that their victims had a hand in the their own rape, and others blame friends or peers. A few rapists explain control and anger as their motivation to rape, while another group describes a god-like supremacy over their victims as their objective. Lastly, some rapists imply that their own fantasy led them to rape.

Predatory rapists explain the role violence played in their attacks as fitting into one of the following categories: nonviolence, intimidation, moderate, limited, and ultimate. While the results show several descriptions of murder and necrophilla, violence was selective and used sparingly by serial rapists. The most frequently mentioned method of victim selection was victim vulnerability. The idea of vulnerability demonstrates that violence in itself may not be a priority for rapists. When rapists think a female could not or would not resist an attack and an opportunity prevailed by circumstance or manipulation, they indeed, attack regardless of the time of day, whose company she's in, her age, or her circumstance. Offenders continually survey their social environments for prey; their target techniques are largely in one of the following categories: easy prey; random; and situational. Mostly, how an offender perceives his potential victim affects his decision to attack, and how she responds during the attack will affect its outcome.

Make no mistake! Predators attack females for the purpose of physical exploitation including sexual contact; they are in the serious business of fulfilling needs. Predators make few mistakes when they hunt down another person especially another person who seems to be vulnerable. The American criminal justice system must seriously deal with these offenders at a mature and responsible level. But, it is recommended that a velvet glove and dagger approach to crime control be considered should America wish to survive the 21st century. That is, effective prevention and persuasive punishment.

Part of the problem is that politically correct arm-chaired thinkers explain heinous criminals such as predatory rapists through exquisite explanations. But controlling criminals is making a lot of hard choices; one of those choices is realizing that politically correct theory has little to do with criminal reality. The fact is that throughout the history of mankind, there have always been predators. Chances are—that's the way it will always be; we can't apprehend them all and even if we did, that doesn't mean they won't strike again. We don't have to become their victims, and we don't have help children become corrupt monsters. Fighting back is the first line of defense for females.

Equally important, I can't help noticing that many serial rapists like most other heinous offenders embrace evil as a motivator or as an excuse to commit unspeakable acts. Due in part to these predatory descriptions, it seems obvious that American society is moving toward both an unhealthy and an unholy society. Many criminals embrace and internalize the evil in the American society which in-turn reinforces and often rewards conduct that hints at societal destruction. I am left wondering if this popular and reinforced image of violent behavior doesn't raise another question much like the ugly head of a cross-eyed creature lurking on a different plane of existence who sees its wickedness through a mask of sanity. Clearly, public violence has become private violence and is heading toward collective violence. Like drug traffickers who claim they give customers what they want, rapists, too, suggest that they supply experiences for their prey to become victims. Fact is many vulnerable females play the role of a victim when attacked. No, I'm not blaming the victim for the attack. I'm saying that females due in part to the media have learned how to play a helpless role when attacked.

Continuing along the line of this thought, America's youth are traumatized by violence and antiseptic misery of the underprivileged. It's fashionable to dress and behave like lower class gangsters. Fear entrepreneurs portray violence and sexual exploitation as an appropriate lifestyle. These fear peddlers maintain oddly enough that serial rapists have the physical and intellectual ability to destroy their victims, and what's more—they want too. The truth is that they are wrong. Women are not helpless or dumb in the light of an attack as most have both the physical ability and the intelligence to end an attack and do so. The edge an offender has over his victim is not physical strength but surprise. Most serial rapists require surprise since most serial rapists are wimps who have no desire for violence. There are a number of rape attempts that were ended by the women who fought back without a gun or a badge.

Certainly, you, too, felt the vulgarity of the predators who feed from the bodies of their victims. Yet, developed societies are obedient societies in the sense of collective consent. They say that the degree of such consent may vary on social setting and consequently the use of coercion to maintain the social order may be more or less noticeable. Therefore, however you say it, law and morals must be preserved should we want to control violent crime. I have presented compelling evidence suggesting that the criminal justice system must become effective and morally spirited should we wish to proceed into the 21st century as a safe society.

Serial rapists are self-indulgent people pursuing objectives without regard for the welfare of others or themselves—or at least that is what they want others to believe. Reading between the lines of their self-reports, it sounds as if they want immediate relief from a their frustrations or if you will indulge me, an itch, and they took the quickest way to relieve themselves—forcible rape much like a junkie takes a hit or an alcoholic takes a drink. How does a society resolve itself of serial rapists especially when something inside that individual pushes him to feed an addiction? Maybe the American Psychological community should classify sexual offenders as addicts! Why is it so hard to entertain the possibility that sexual offenders are addicted to sexual attacks? It is a matter of record that some sexual offenders have been medically treated with depo-provera (female hormones) and some of those offenders seem to respond favorably. It's called chemical castration. Recently the state of California passed a law injecting pedophiles with depo-provera to reduce their sexual drives by reducing their testosterone levels. They all won't respond positively to the drug, but understanding that serial rapists like most sexual offenders can never be rehabilitated, society must try different methods of control. Frankly, the best minds of our day want to debate the political correctness of sexual offenders and put those offenders into psychological or sociological categories to explain why they, too, were allegedly victimized as youngsters or adults instead of supporting serious methods of control.

We all have our Calvaries; yet, sexual offenders are exactly where they want to be in their lives, doing actually what they want to do. They rape to feel comfortable with themselves and the world around them. Serial rape is nourishment, and without it, they feel that they would suffocate and die. The more they rape, they greater number of rapes necessary to satisfy their appetite. Once imprisoned, they go through a physical and psychological process that resembles the withdrawal experiences of drug addicts. They may rape in prison, but since their victims are men, their appetite is rarely satisfied. The itch is on the roof of a Mack transfer track, and as it runs over the chest of a rapist, he tries to scratch. Maybe a medical model of confinement might be helpful if its operators would remember that their clients are predators and not victims and that the likelihood of them curing these monsters will never happen. Let's hope for control!

The criminal justice community must come to the realization that they can not control crime alone. They must also realize by now that they should make the community an equal partner in crime control. All sexual offenders must be identified to the community, and kept out of sensitive jobs near children and other vulnerable type individuals. But above all, police and community crime control prerogatives must be enhanced, plea-bargaining must be eliminated, mandatory life sentences must be initiated, and capital punishment should be an immediate consequence (after one appeal) of all newly convicted chronic sexual offenders.

Part I: References

Alpert, G.P., & Dunham, R.G. (1997). *Policing urban America.* Prospect Heights, IL: Waveland Press.

Amir, M. (1971). *Patterns in forcible rape.* Chicago: University of Chicago Press.

Athens, L.H. (1980). *Violent criminal acts and actors.* Boston: Routledge & Kegan Paul.

Averill, J.R. (1993). Illusions of anger. In R.B. Felson and J.T. Tedeschi (Eds.). *Aggression and Violence: Social Interactionist Perspectives.* (Pp. 171-192). Washington DC: APA.

Bandura, A.(1973). *Aggression: A social learning process.* Englewood Cliffs, NJ: Prentice Hall.

Bart, P. & O'Brien, P. (1985). *Stopping rape: Successful survival strategies.* Elmsford, NY: Pergamon Press.

Becker, H. & Geer, B. (1957). Participant observation and interviewing: A comparison. *Sociology of Applied Anthropology, 16,* 76-82.

Berger, P.L. (1963). *Invitation to sociology: A humanistic perspective.* NY: Doubleday.

Belknap, J. (1996). *The invisible woman: Gender, crime, and justice.* NY: Wadsworth.

Blumer. H. (1969). *Symbolic interactionism.* Englewood Cliffs, NJ: Prentice Hall.

Brownmiller, S. (1975). *Against our will: Men, women, and rape.* NY: Simon & Schuster.

Bureau of Justice Statistics. (1997). *Sourcebook of criminal justice statistics-1994.* Washington DC: U.S. Department of Justice, Office of Justice Programs.

Cohen, M., Garofalo, R, Boucher, R., & Seghorn, T. (1971). The psychology of rapists. *Seminars in Psychiatry, 3,* 307-327.

Denno, D. (1990). *Biology and Violence: From birth to adulthood.* NY: Cambridge University Press.

Douglas, J., & Olshaker, M. (1995). *Mind hunter.* NY: Pocket Star Books.

Ellis, L. 1989. *Theories of rape.* New York: Hemisphere.

Eysenck, H.,& Gudjonsson, G. (1989). *The causes and cures of criminality.* NY: Plenum.

Felson, R.B., & Krohn, M. (1990). Motives for rape. *Journal of Research in Crime and Delinquency, 27* (3), 222-241.

Gaskins, D. "Pee Wee" with Wilton, E. (1994). *Final truth.* NY: Windsor.

Gibbons, D.C. (1992). *Society, crime, and criminal behavior.* Englewood Cliffs, NJ: Simon & Schuster.

Glaser, B., & Strauss, A. (1967). *The discovery of the grounded theory: Strategies for qualitative research.* Chicago: Aldine.

Goldstein, A.P. (1990). *Delinquents on delinquency.* Champaign, IL: Research Press.

Gordon, M.T., & Riger, S. (1989). *The female fear: The social cost of rape.* NY: Free.

Gollmar, R. (1981). *America's most bizarre murderer: Edward Gein.* NY: Pinnacle.

Gottfredson, M., & Hirschi, T. (1990). *A general theory of crime.* Stanford, CA: Stanford.

Groth, N.A. (1979). *Men who rape: The psychology of the offender.* NY: Plenum Press.

Groth, N.A., & Burgess, A.W. (1980). Male rape: Offenders and victims. *American Journal of Psychiatry,* 137(7), 806-810.

Hazelwood, R., & Warren, J. (1990). Rape: The criminal behavior of the serial rapist. *FBI Law Enforcement Bulletin.* February, pp. 11-15.

Hazelwood R., Reboussin,R., & Warren, J. (1989). Serial rape: Correlates of increased aggression and the relationship of offender pleasure to victim resistance. *Journal of Interpersonal Violence* 4(1), 65-78.

Heller, A., Stamatiou, W., & Puntscher-Riekmann, S. (1993). The limits to natural law and the paradox of evil. *Journal fur Sozialforschung, 33*(2), 107-120.

Holmes, R. (1991). *Sex crimes.* CA: Sage.

Kanin, E. J. (1984). Date rape: Unofficial criminals and victims. *Victimology 9,* 95-108.

Katz, Jack. (1988). *Seductions of Crime.* NY: Basic Books.

Katz, Fred E. (1993). *Ordinary People and Extraordinary Evil.* NY: State University of NY.

Kruttschnitt, C., Ward, D., & Sheble, M. A. (1987). Abuse-resistant youth: Some factors that may inhibit violent criminal behavior. *Social Forces,66*(2), 501-519.

Lyman, Stanford. (1978). Seven Deadly Sins: Society and Evil. NY: St.Martin's.

MacKinnon, C. (1987). *Feminism unmodified.* NY: Wiley.

Medea, A. ,& Thompson, K. (1974). *Against rape: A survival manual for women: How to cope with rape physically and emotionally.* NY: Farrar, Straus, and Giraux.

Palmer, C.T. (1988). Twelve reasons why rape is not sexually motivated: A skeptical examination. *Journal of Sex Research, 25* (5), 12-30.

Petersilia, J. (1977). *Criminal careers of habitual felons: A summary report.* Santa Monica, CA: Rand.

Pinilla-Esteban, D.L.H. (1993). Public violence and private violence. *Revista Internacional de Sociologia, 5,* 163-173.

Quinsey, V.S., Chaplin, T.S., & Upfold, D. (1984). Sexual arousal to nonsexual violence and sadomasochistic themes among rapists and nonsexual offenders. *Journal of Consulting Clinical Psychology, 52,* 651-657.

Reid, S.T. (1996). *Crime and criminology.* Madison, WI: Brown & Benchmark.

Reiman, Jeffrey. (1995). *The rich get richer and the poor get prison.* NY: Macmillan.

Rule, A. (1980). *The stranger beside me.* NY: New American Library.

Sanday, P. (1981). The socio-cultural context of rape: A cross cultural study. *Journal of Social Issues, 37,* 5-27.

Samenow, S. (1984). *Inside the criminal mind.* NY: Random.

Schmalleger, F. (1979). World of the career criminal. *Human Nature,* 2, 53-57.

Schmalleger, F. (1997). *Criminology today.* Englewood Cliffs, NJ: Prentice Hall.

Schwendinger, J., & Schwendinger, H. (1983). *Rape and inequality.* Beverly Hills: Sage Publications.

Scully, D., & Marolla, J. (1984). Convicted rapists' vocabulary of motive: Excuses and justifications. *Social Problems, 31,* 530-544.

Scully, D. (1990). *Understanding sexual violence.* NY: Putnum.

Stevens, D.J. (1998a). Interviews with women convicted of murder: Battered women syndrome revisited. *International Review of Victimology,* 6(2), 117-135.

Stevens, D.J. (1998b). The impact of time-served and regime on prisoners' anticipation of crime: Female Prisonisation Effects. *The Howard Journal of Criminal Justice, 37*(2), 188-205.

Stevens, D.J. (1998c). Attitudes of police officers about their jobs: A study of trust, discretion, and training. *International Police Chief Review.* In Press.

Stevens, D.J. (1997a). Violence and serial rape. *Journal of Police and Criminal Psychology.* 12(1), 39-47.

Stevens, D.J. (1997b). Prison regime and drugs. *The Howard Journal of Criminal Justice, 36*(1), 14-27.

Stevens, D.J. (1997c). Influences of early childhood experiences on subsequent criminally violent behavour. *Studies on crime and crime prevention, 6*(1), 34-50.

Stevens, D.J. (1997d). Prisoner Restrictions, Inmate Custodial Relations, and Inmate Attitudes Towards Compliance. *Research and Statistics Branch of the Correctional Service of Canada.*

Stevens, D.J. (1997g). Communities and homicide: Why blacks resort to murder. *The Criminologist, 21*(3), 145-157.

Stevens, D.J. (1995a). Motives of serial rapists. *Free Inquiry of Creative Sociology, 23*(2), 117-127.

Stevens, D.J. (1995b). The impact of time served and custody level on offender attitudes. *Forum on Corrections Research, 9,* 12-14.

Stevens, D.J. (1994a). Predatory rape and victim targeting techniques." *The Social Science Journal, 31* (4), 421-433.

Stevens, D.J. (1994b). The depth of imprisonment and prisonisation: Levels of security and prisoners' anticipation of future violence. *The Howard Journal of Criminal Justice, 33* (2), 137-157.

Stevens, D.J. (1992a). Research Note: The death sentence and inmate attitudes. *Crime & Delinquency, 38,* 272-279.

Stevens, D. J. (1992b). Examining inmate attitudes: Do prisons deter crime? *The State of Corrections-American Correctional Association: 1991.* 272-279.

Stevens, D.J. (1988). Education: The Assembly. *Urban Education, 23* (1), 107-114.

Sussman L., & Bordwell, S. (1981). *The rapist file.* NY: Chelsea House.

Tock, H., & Adams, K. (1989). *The disturbed violent offender.* New Haven, MA: Yale University Press.

Thomas, W.I., & Thomas, D. (1928). *The child in America: Behavior problems and programs.* NY: Knopf.

Weiner, N.A., Zahn, M.A., & Sagi, R.J. (1990). *Violence: Patterns, causes, public policy.* FL: Harcourt Race Jovanovich Publishers.

Zimbardo, P.G. (1972). Pathology of imprisonment. *Society, 9,* 4-8.

Zukier, H. (1994). The twisted road to genocide: On the psychological development of evil during the Holocaust. *Social Research, 61* (2), 423-455.

Part II

CHAPTER 11

A Case Study of Three Generations of Predatory Sexual Offenders

Introduction

There are few studies describing the past experiences of incarcerated sexual offenders. One aim of this paper is to bridge the gap in the literature concerning what appears to be a hidden phenomena with the hopes that researchers will professionally study sexual offenders with a similar objectivity as they have other offenders. Perhaps one reason sexual offenders are rarely studied may be that there is a great deal of confusion about the lifestyles and motives of sexual offenders in the first place regardless whether they're confined or not. For instance, the motives of sexual offenders have been politicized by some writers to further specific agendas often times at the expense of aiding offenders to control their conduct (Jenkins, 1994; Thornhill & Palmer, 2000, Toch & Adams, 1994; Stevens, 1998a). Some researchers suggest that rape in general can be viewed as a sexual act with its roots in evolution (Thornhill & Palmer, 2000). One mission of many predatory sexual offenders is sexual intimacy (MacKinnon, 1987; Scully, 1990; Stevens, 1998a). Continuing along this line of reasoning, sexual assault it is claimed, is not a sexual act but normal male behavior motivated to maintain dominance and power over women and often to accommodate their fantasy, anger, and sadistic objectives (Brownmiller, 1975; Groth, 1980).[42] Nonetheless, it is strongly suggested that the personality of a violent offender is a product of biological inheritance, culture, environment, and common and unique experiences (Holmes & Holmes, 1996; Stevens, 1998a).

One starting point to examine crime and the prediction of dangerousness of violent offenders might be that crime itself is a form of deviant behavior measured by certain established standards of society (Carter & Radelet, 1999). The nature of criminal acts is the use and/or the threat of force or fraud. Of equal concern, individuals vary in their propensity to use criminal force and fraud (Gottfredson & Hirschi, 1990).[43] Each of us has a unique way of relating to others, through a set of values and attitudes. Therefore, each of us has a unique personality (Holmes & Holmes, 1996). But, attitude including personality and its impact on behavioral patterns may be variables that are more unrelated than expected.

Psychopaths and Antisocial Personality Disorders

Behavioral experts including the FBI often report that psychopathic personalities are causal factors of sexually violent behavior (Douglas & Olshaker, 1995; Pallone & Hennessy, 1992). A sexual predator might

---

42. Gottfredson and Hirschi (1990) further argue that most crime is trivial and mundane resulting in little loss and few gains. In fact, these authors argue that "these (criminal acts) are events whose temporal and spatial distributions are highly predictable, that require little preparation, leave few lasting consequences, and often do not produce the result intended by the offender (1990, p.16)."

43. Gottfredson and Hirschi (1990) further argue that most crime is trivial and mundane resulting in little loss and few gains. In fact, these authors argue that "these (criminal acts) are events whose temporal and spatial distributions are highly predictable, that require little preparation, leave few lasting consequences, and often do not produce the result intended by the offender (1990, p.16)."

possess some of the characteristics of a psychopath or be diagnosed as an individual with antisocial personality disorder (ASPD) characteristics. That is, a psychopath and/or an ASPD personality can be similarly defined as a self centered person who has not been properly socialized into pro-social attitudes and values. They have developed little sense of right and wrong and have little empathy with others. Also, they are incapable of feeling remorse or guilt from misconduct (Akers, 1997; APA, 1994; Samenow, 1984).[44] Yet, there are significant distinctions between ASPD and psychopathy to mental health and criminal justice systems. The FBI described ASPD personalities as an individual who displays a sense of entitlement, unremorseful, apathetic to others, unconscionable, blameful of others, manipulative and conning, effectively cold, disparate understanding of behavior and socially acceptable behavior, disregardful of social obligations, nonconforming to social norms, and irresponsible (Hare, 1996). But chronic sexual violent offenders are not simply persistently antisocial individuals who met DSM-IV criteria for ASPD, they are psychopaths-remorseless predators who use charm, intimidation and, if necessary, impulsive and cold-blooded violence to attain their ends (Hare, 1996).[45] Unfortunately, it is a distinction that is often blurred, not only in the minds of many clinicians, but in the latest edition of DSM-IV,

---

44. See APA (1994) for a closer look at Antisocial Personality Disorder which includes in its diagnostic criteria (301.7, pp. 649): a pervasive pattern of disregard for and violation of the rights of others and failure to conform to social norms with respect to lawful behaviors as indicated by repeatedly performing acts that are grounds for arrest; deceitfulness, impulsivity, aggressiveness, irresponsibility, and a lack of remorse. Also see Narcissistic Personality Disorder which seems to add to a psychopathic definition.

45. Gary Heidnik who electrocuted one women while she stood in a pool of water by pushing an electrical cord against her and tortured and killed many others in the basement of his home might illustrate a specific example a psychotic predator (Schmalleger, 1999).

says Hare (1996). This paper must acknowledge that there are experts who continue to argue that predictions of predators can be largely causal through physical attributes such as damaged frontal lobes (Raine, et al, 1994) and that personality assessment instruments such as the Millon Clinical Multiaxial Inventory (MCMI) and beyond can help define personality profiles of confined offenders (Weeks & Morison, 1993).[46]

Most cold-blooded murderers meet the criteria for ASPD, despite the fact that most individuals with ASPD are not psychopaths (Hare, 1996). An unfortunate consequence of the ambiguity inherent in DSM-IV is likely to be a court case in which one clinician says a defendant meets the DSM-IV definition of ASPD, another clinician says he does not, and both are right. The first clinician uses only the formal diagnostic criteria whereas the second clinician agrees that the defendant meets the formal criteria but argues that he or she does not have the personality traits described in the "Associated Features" section of the DSM-IV text (Hare, 1996). Confusion continues. ASPD is very common in criminal populations, and those with the disorder are heterogeneous with respect to personality, attitudes and motivations for engaging in criminal behavior.

Incarceration of Sexual Offenders

In 1980, state prisons held 20,500 sex offenders. By 1994, over 88,000 sex offenders were held in state prisons, and in 1998 that number was close to 100,000 (Bureau of Justice Statistics (BJS), 1999). Then, too, 60% of the 234,000 convicted sex offenders were on parole or probation

---

46. Suppose an inmate can't read or write as well as expected. My own research shows that since the level of education in prison is far less than the national average that inmates have to be read simple questions from a questionnaire in order to answer a closed-ended response such as yes or no so therefore, what methods were taken to protect validity? (Stevens, 1994).

in 1994 (U.S. Department of Justice (USDOJ), 1999a). About 234,000 convicted sex offenders are under the care, custody, or control of corrections agencies on an average day (Greenfield, 1997). Nearly 60% are under conditional supervision in the community. A national survey in 1992 found that every year 683,000 women are forcibly raped, and rape has an annual victim cost of $127 billion excluding child sex abuse followed by assault at $93 billion (USDOJ, 1999b).

After being sentenced to prison, an inmate is transported to a diagnostic or reception center and undergoes a classification process. This process can determine an inmate's security level and rehabilitative needs. That is, where and under what security conditions an inmate will be confined. Largely, variables such as seriousness of offense, institutional conduct, the possibility of escape, and the potential for violent behavior are examined. Most states do not have a specific institution for each level of security and often the facilities are divided into sections (maximum, medium, and minimum are examples) for different categories. Classification of inmates was originally regarded as the diagnostic method necessary to assess the treatment needs of offenders. However, the existence and function of rehabilitative programs continues to be challenged by the public who demands a punitive approach towards inmates especially sexual offenders. In most correctional systems, sexual offenders are considered high risk regardless of the severity of their conviction record, which in some states can include offenses such as public exposure (for example, Massachusetts). However, there are vast differences between a chronic predatory sexual offender and/or other sexual offenders (Toch & Adams, 1994; Stevens, 1998a). One purpose of this paper is to examine the experiences of incarcerated biologically related sexual offenders who characterized violent sexual attacks on others.

Methodology

The sample largely consisted of seven individual family members (see Appendix 1:

Stephen's Genogram). The eldest named Stephen was approximately 52 at the time of the interviews. He was incarcerated in South Carolina and a college student at the prison where the researcher instructed classes over a two year period. Stephen had three sons: Milton 34, Henry George 29, and Collin 23. Milton was a free man living in Jackson, Florida. He had 18 year old twins, named Larry and Tamera. Larry was incarcerated in New York. He plea-bargained two Class E Felonies (sexual assault of a minor) and 1 Class A Felony (sodomy) for a four year (no probation) prison sentence. Tamera was recently released from an Illinois prison where she served six months for prostitution, aggravated assault, and possession of an illicit substance presumably heroin. Milton had two other children but did not know their whereabouts. Stephen's second son, Henry George was incarcerated in New York and his third son Collin was confined in South Carolina along with his father. Collin was a respondent along with his father in an earlier study conducted at the prison in South Carolina, although Collin was not a student of the researcher. Henry George had a 15 year old son, Jason, who was adjudicated to a juvenile center in Ohio.

Herein are the accounts of these family members although fictitious names and locations were used throughout this paper to protect both participants and victims of the participants. Also, the respondent's dialogues were edited when editing would not change the meaning of those descriptions. The respondents were advised that there were no incentives of any kind for their participation. Although the respondents had little incentive to lie about their experiences, they were chronic criminals, and criminals lie about everything. It should also be acknowledged that many individuals construct events in ways that are acceptable to their audiences and/or offer accounts about past events grounded in present expectations (Lyman

& Scott, 1989). The reputation of the researcher as a prison teacher, holding the confidence of high custody offenders played a role in the events. Each interview lasted 2 to 3 hours and each participant met with the researcher two to three times, except for Stephen who talked about himself with the researcher at length while the instructor awaited other students to arrive at class. After each meeting, data were entered into a computer grind. Data were collected over a four year period of time and in various settings including prison visiting rooms, educational centers, and in restaurants. There are 110 pages of text produced from those interviews. The cities where the interviews took place were in located is Georgia, Florida, Ohio, New York, North Carolina, and South Carolina. This study utilized a grounded theory approach to understanding the data. That is, data collection and analysis proceeded simultaneously in keeping with Grasser and Strauss (1967) perspectives of ground theory. Both the process and products of research were shaped through the data. The researcher has successfully used this approach in other studies involving high risk offenders (Stevens, 1998a; 1998b).

Lastly, the descriptions are intended to be illustrative examples as opposed to case reports. Furthermore, this paper should not be looked upon as a final or a "last word" on sexual offenders, as the writer considers this paper only as a "work in progress" and will act merely as a reference to further research.

Findings

Taking Earle and Earle's (1995) lead, a genogram was developed to better examine the three generational experiences of the King family. A genogram is a graphic representation using a family systems approach in examining an offenders family members, family rules, and family dynamics. Its strength comes from the opportunity to see at a glance, history, experiences, and perceptions of an individual's history, say Earle and Earle (1995).

Stephen King

When Stephen was 11 or 12, his parents divorced. What he remembered most about them was that they were always fighting with each other and that his father drunk heavily especially with Stephen's uncles and aunts. He recalled one Christmas when "good times" were expressed by his father as depending on how many bottles of whisky the family emptied in one setting. Stephen's mother liked his favorite uncle, Max who was the youngest of his father's three brothers. Often Max and his mother embraced much to his father's distaste resulting in angry words and slammed doors behind exiting relatives. Years later, Stephen learned that his mother had several sexual relationships, most of whom were far younger men than his father. He never learned if one of her lovers was Max. He never saw Max after the divorce of his parents. His younger brother and he lived with their mother for a year or two until she died. Then they moved with his father who was never home. The state took custody of Stephen when he 15 and his brother and placed them both in separate foster homes. Stephen reported that that home was "heaven" for him. He was happy there primarily because it was peaceful. But his brother was successful in running away.

This finding is consistent with earlier research revealing that frequent parental quarreling was a more frightening experience for a convicted violent felon than other early childhood experiences (Stevens, 1997b). One implication of those findings was that parents who continually quarrel steer a child to immediate gratification and loss of self-control bringing that child towards future violence.

As a youth, Stephen masturbated often, sometimes twice a day. "It filled a empty space in my head and it made me feel better," he said. At 15, Stephen often visited prostitutes both those who worked the streets and those who worked the parlors at least once a month.

At 18, he joined the military or faced jail time for the sexual assault of Andrea Evert, his 13 year girl friend. That union produced his first son,

Milton. In the military, Stephen completed two tours of duty in Southeast Asia. He was honorably discharged at 21. He lived in Atlanta for several months before moving in with Andrea Evert and Milton Evert who lived with her grandparents in rural South Carolina. This researcher got the impression from Stephen and other family members that Andrea was not in agreement with his moving into her family home but was powerless to stop him.

His first prison sentence was for aggravated assault when he was 23. He, as opposed to the prosecutor, plea-bargained it down from the crime of rape to assault. During the diagnostic process, he was assigned to a minimum security prison. However, there was a considerable discussion about his military experiences which the classification processor dwelled upon. The participant said that the classification workers were fascinated by his war stories and other correctional personnel joined the discussions often leaving inmates at their classification's desks.

Stephen's life in prison was uneventful and he worked during the day on road projects. However, it was at this prison that he met Lindsey Truman, a correctional officer. They were sexually involved and would live together, now and again, over the next thirty years.

His second prison sentence was for sexual assault. During the classification process old records were examined and he was confined again to a minimum facility until he attacked and raped an elderly female church volunteer. Nothing came of the attack except he was transferred to a high custody facility.

Stephen's third conviction was for aggravated assault. During his classification process, Stephen revealed to the intake officer that Stephen was an alcoholic in order to be assigned to AA meetings during his sentence. He explained to the researcher that he was not an alcoholic but wanted to attend the meetings. In order to attend AA or any other rehab type encounters, it had to be listed on the incoming diagnostic reports. This information is general knowledge to most experienced inmates, so they would establish their "prison identity" during classification.

During interviews with the principal researcher, Stephen's descriptions characterized experiences that revealed licentiously driven motives as a sexual offender. Prior to his attacks, he made conscious assessments about his victims. He thought about what he would receive from those attacks, and on a few occasions, he fantasized about them prior to the actual attack. What Stephen wanted most was sexual intimacy. It didn't matter how he got it or with whom. For instance, when he gained access to a parking lot that connected to a high rise condominium, here's how he described that attack:

> The ol'e guy saw me and I was polite. I helped them into the elevator and touched her…and…while holding her up. Not bad, I remember thinking. I decided I'd screw her if I could….. He passed out in the living room, and I poured her into bed. I think she pushed me away, but I held her hands with one hand and pulled her skirt up. Her…smelled, but it welcomed my…and it seemed forever but I finally came [ejaculated]. He suddenly appeared and started hitting me. I shoved him. He kept on com'en. When I ran out, I forgot my shoes.

Several times, Stephen received oral sex from a prostitute, attacked a female and sometimes raped her, went home, and masturbated in the bathroom all in the same day. During all three of these activities, the only time he was erect was during the sexual assaults. He explained, however, that he had committed rape because he felt guilty as a result of his encounter with a prostitute. "In the john (bathroom), I make it all wash away (when I masturbated)," said he. He didn't clean himself between encounters and remarked that he enjoyed the "taste of hooker and sweetie (the individual raped) on my hands" (he would wet his hands by licking them as he would masturbate). At this writing, Stephen has been released from prison.

Stephen King had two brothers. One was 12 years older, and Sam was 2 years younger than Stephen. His oldest brother died in an automobile accident. Stephen learned that his brother was drunk at the time of the accident. His younger brother, Sam, ran away from a foster home at age 14. Years later, Stephen learned that Sam finished high school, worked as a laborer for a furniture company and later became a truck driver. He went to college at night, earned a degree, and taught 8th grade biology. Sam lived with his wife and 3 children in Memphis. Apparently, he was never involved in criminal behavior. Although Stephen said that Sam run his family with an "iron fist." When asked about that, Stephen replied raising his fist, "Ya know. He takes no shit from that woman or he'd kick her ass."

Andrea Evert

Andrea Evert, the mother of Stephen's first child, Milton, was living with another man in Georgia at the time of this study. She had three additional children, none of whom were fathered by Stephen. What was known about Andrea Evert was offered by Stephen and Milton who were generally informed of her activities by friends. Andrea Evert had a highly antagonistic personality when she was drunk, which was most of the time, and she was a known thief. When Andrea was sober, she found "Jesus and christianity" again and moved from her home. She would move with another man—"a christian man. But when things got, ya know, routine," she returned to alcohol and retail store theft and left the church and everything she owned behind," reported Milton. By most counts, she experienced at least five complete changes in her life: each time changing homes, personal belongings, and family members. Her last known address was Georgia where she frequently attended the Macon Baptist Church. She was on probation. Andrea never visited Stephen while he was incarcerated, but telephoned Milton every so often no matter where she lived to inquire about Milton and her grandchildren. Milton made it clear, however, that his mother was not welcomed in his home because she was "too free with her hands on my children. I'll never forgive her." Milton would not elaborate any further on those thoughts.

Milton Evert

Milton Evert was 34 and had only lived with Stephen approximately 2-3 years during his youth (the balance of the time, Stephen was incarcerated or living with Lindsey Truman). Milton Evert was never arrested, gainfully employed as a plumber, and lived with his wife of 17 years, Norma in Jacksonville, Florida. They met in high school and married the summer of their graduation. Norma has worked for Walmart for the past 15 years and rose to a managerial position. Milton and Norma seem well adjusted with each other. They were homeowners, church goers, and they were on bowling league together. The researcher met Milton and Norma during a their prison visit to the educational area when Stephen King graduated from the academic program with a college degree. But, it would not be for three years before the researcher would visit with Milton after that initial meeting due to correctional regulation and a luck of interest on the part of the researcher. When the researcher learned that Milton's son, Larry Evert, was apprehended for sexual assault, he telephoned Milton and later visited Larry while he was confined in a NY jail. From that discussion and a subsequent personal visit with Milton, the researcher got the impression that Milton and Norma were an agreeable, nonjudgmental couple. For instance, when the researcher asked how it felt to have a daddy who was a prisoner, Milton said, "We all got our priorities." When asked about his twin children's criminal activities, Milton reported that "we all have our own way of doing things." Milton and Norma had one set of twins: Larry Evert and Tamara Evert. They also had one other son who was 15. They did not know the youngest son's whereabouts.

Larry Evert

Larry Evert was 17. He finished high school a year earlier than most youngsters by attending summer school. Nonetheless, he was recently incarcerated in a New York prison at the time of this study (Fall, 1999). Then, too, Larry Evert was highly aggressive during the interviews with this researcher, and a few correctional officers described what characterized Larry as possessing a combative and antagonistic attitude. For instance, when an officer told Larry to stop for a personal search, Larry swore at him and called him a racist. "Inmates don't conduct themselves that'a way, Mister," the officer told him. Another officer told the researcher when he was leaving that Larry would "run his mouth all the time if we let'em." What was learned during the interview between Larry Evert and the researcher can not all be stated in detail due in part to space limitations and in part to the newness of his conviction (other charges were pending). Many of Larry's descriptions can be characterized as sexual aggression towards females. For example, Larry described a physical attack upon a 14 year old girl who refused his sexual advances during a different epode of sexual activity other than the one conviction he already ready received. Larry reported that he knew "what girls want and I know how to convince them they're right." He laughed after making that statement. Larry made little effort to hide his attitude about females and how they should serve males. "There's only one time a babe should open her mouth, and that's to hag on my joint," he said.

Larry reported that sometimes it seemed as if he were in "a dream" during sexual activities. Time slipped by. For instance, when he began his assault it might have been noon and the next moment it was three o'clock. "It never felt very long…ya know, ten minutes maybe fifteen, but damn, time got away from me. One time, I started at 11 at night and the next thing I realized was that the sun was coming up." (Note: this is a similar observation made by the other participants in this study. It is also a different time experience from other nonpredator sexual offenders who talk in terms of an attack lasting a few minutes).

He said what pushed him towards sexual activity was largely "because that's what I want. The thrill, man, strictly the thrill." Experience with similar offenders guides one interpretation of his thoughts (and other typical thoughts he shared): Larry held a mind-set about crime. That is, he was aware of what he wanted and aware of what he had to do to get it and little else mattered. Yet, he was never able to articulate why he wanted to sexually attack someone—that is, why the compulsion to continually experience the "thrill of it all." One perspective is that he had trouble with an explanation because he couldn't understand the significance or the consequences of his behavior, and, he didn't care if he did know.[47] It may be interesting to note that many criminally violent offenders understand their agenda and how to satisfy it. This thought is consistent with writers who argue that many violent offenders decide to commit violent crime centered in a single perspective: acquiring the benefits of crime (Gottfredson & Hirschi, 1990; Samenow, 1984). Then, too, convenience and opportunity can act as a trigger for individuals who lack self-control, are impulsive, insensitive, physical, risk takers, and shortsighted (Gottfredson & Hirschi, 1990). All of which might help shape Larry's conduct. "When I looked at da' little hoe' (the 10 year old girl he attacked), I knew she'd be a mean piece," Larry confirmed.

Larry implied that he "experimented" with a male but didn't like it. He also reported that he enjoyed sexual movies, had sexual "tools" (i.e.dildos), and sexually explicit pictures of young girls and boys. In the experience of the researcher, these items are rarely typical of a 17 year old. Furthermore,

---

47. The researcher does not pretend to understand what's in the mind of another individual, but he can observe and objectively report the conduct of others. These remarks, like many other remarks throughout this paper, are merely feelings the researcher had during interviews. They are offered to aid the reader in an observation that was made at the time of the interview.

Larry did not smoke or use drugs. Larry would not comment about masturbation practices. The district attorney called Larry a sexual predator. He wanted Larry incarcerated for a maximum prison sentence for a sexual conviction. But the DA apparently felt there wasn't enough evidence to convict Larry for the rape of a 10 year old child who Larry had babysat while visiting his mother's brother in NY (this is whom Larry referred to as a "mean piece"). Thus, a deal were struck whereby Larry plea-bargained two Class E Felonies (sexual assault of a minor) and one Class A Felony (sodomy) for four years, no probation. He will be released with good behavior, in about 8 months.

Larry was told that he would undergo extensive psychological testing because of his sexual conviction but the case worker told Larry that he was not sure when that would happen. When Larry was apprehended there was considerable media attention to his case. He sat in the county jail for three months before trail but was on lock down most of the time. Once convicted, he was transferred several times in three weeks to four different prisons throughout the state until he arrived at the prison where he would serve out his time. Because of his age and his offense he was in protective custody (PC) and locked down twenty-three and a half hours a day except for the visits of the researcher. Finally, after a few months he was assigned a bed. He revealed that one of the correctional officers discovered he was a sexual offender (SO) and told other officers about him. One afternoon when the cell block of young offenders was empty except for Larry, four officers entered the cell block and confronted Larry. "Are you a SO?" they asked. "I asked how they came to that conclusion," Larry wrote (in a letter to the researcher). "They didn't answer but I could figure. So I turned the scales on them and produced a piece of paper saying I am enrolled in the ASAT program (Alcohol, Substance Abuse Treatment). If the CO who told you that I was a SO was right, then what's this paper about?…DOC is mandated to treat the nature of the prison charge before any subsequent element and something about they can be sued if they didn't. The believed it. How can you trust a CO, I asked. I knew that piece of paper would come in handy."

Lindsey Truman

Lindsey Truman was a correctional officer at the first prison where Stephen was confined, almost thirty years prior to this study. Once released, they lived together. When the authorities learned of Stephen and Lindsey's arrangement, they fired her. The two of them had been sexually involved prior to his release from prison, some correctional personnel rumors reported. Stephen would not comment on those rumors, but other inmates often made jokes about Stephen and a correctional officer.

Lindsey was far younger than Stephen, "and a devoted Christian woman," he added. She had a highly aggressive nature in that she was referred to as a "control freak" by her son Collin. "She has to know every-thing that's going on, but she never offended anyone," explained her other son, Henry George. The data implied that Lindsey possessed a rigid per-sonality and placed demands on Stephen that he could not keep. One of those demands was that he stop criminal activity.[48] He apparently broke his promise as evidenced by his reincarceration. One guess is that she never really had any power over him since Stephen was a predator and she was an uneducated woman whose life revolved around Stephen and her church. She also lived in the past and spoke often, Henry George reported, about her earlier marriages which lasted less than a year each. No

---

48. Knowing Stephen, the researcher will speculate that while incarcerated, he manipulated Lindsey into a sexual relationship as it served his purpose at the time. Moving in with her was also to his advantage since Andrea had already left him. Thus, he had no where to go, once released. One of his ploys was to allow others their belief that they were in control, but he has the skill of a predator and knows how to use "control freaks" to his advantage as the researcher witnessed throughout his two years of instructing at the prison where Stephen was an inmate and student.

children were produced from those earlier marriages. Stephen and Lindsey Truman had two sons: Henry George Truman and Collin Truman. It isn't clear when she died, but every family member ignored any conversation about her death. There were indicators that Lindsey and Stephen bitterly fought often with each other over trivia things such as which television shows to watch, Henry George offered during an interview.

Henry George Truman

Henry George Truman was somewhat different than the others in that sex might not have been a preoccupation for him. At least, a sexual dialogue was not part of his conversations during the interviews, and the correctional personnel whom the researcher talked to about Henry George, did not mention sex and/or sexual violations linked to him. He was 29, and the interview took place in the visiting room of the prison. He was divorced twice and presently married to a third wife. His personality seemed low keyed and agreeable. The way one officer described Henry George was "laid back. God almighty, that man could stand next to a explod'en bomb, and he ain't go'en fuss." During the interview with Henry George, when a correctional officer told him to show him his hands, he produced them without a thought and thanked the officer after the encounter. Henry George responded slowly when discussing himself, apparently thinking through his answers before he answered. Prison records revealed Henry George to be an alcoholic and a gambler, but he volunteered that during the interview without a blink. He was convicted of armed robbery while at a poker game. He had been arrested a dozen times for minor violations and convicted once before for assault receiving one year probation as a result. Henry George said he loved his parents, especially his daddy, Stephen. "Why's that?" the researcher asked. "Well, sir, mainly cause I understand him. When mom and pops fought, she'd be the one throw'en shit at him and sometimes it would be head'en right for me. Dad would jump in its path. He sort'a protected my butt." Henry

George reported that his parents fought often and that his parents were both at fault but that Stephen had never "smacked my ole' lady cause he was a gentleman."

"One time I had fifty thousand dollars in front of me from my winnings." The researcher commented, "You said you never really won a lot of money?" Henry George responded, "Lost it. It was seven in the evening when I won. What was I to do the rest of the night? It ain't the money as to why I gamble. Hell, winning—losing—ain't got noth'en to do with it. It's playing that counts." Henry George and his second divorced wife and three children: Jason, 14 was in a juvenile center in North Carolina. They also had a 13 year old daughter and a 10 year old son both of whom lived with his divorced wife. She and the children would visit Henry George every other week while he was incarcerated. To hear Henry George tell it, it was as if they were a happily married couple. A correctional officer implied that "From what I've seen, Henry George's ole' old lady can't keep her hands off'em when she visits. Same thing when the man's wife comes here. That man's got it go'en on."

There were experiences that Henry George shared concerning his incarceration such as he gambled all the time with other inmates and sometimes with correctional personnel. He made alcohol in his cell and had a study supply of drugs. He implied that he received contraband from staff as opposed to correctional officers. This thought is consistent with earlier findings where in many high custody penitentiaries case workers, psychologists, and staff were sources of illicit substances for inmates (Stevens, 1997c).

Collin Truman

Collin was the son of Stephen King and Lindsey Truman and had kept his mother's formal name, like Henry George, since his parents never married. Collin had been divorced at age 21, he said, but his records revealed that he was still married to Mary Allen Quick from Charleston, South Carolina.[49] During interviews with Stephen for an earlier study, he revealed concern for his son Collin Truman who was incarcerated in a minimum custody prison in South Carolina. He was 23 at the time of two personal interviews with the researcher. One of those interviews was conducted in the visiting room of the prison and the other was conducted in the educational center of the prison. Stephen had little knowledge of Collin's criminal history primarily because he never stayed home with Collin's mother and they only lived together between Stephen's prison episodes much like that of his other children. Collin was not aware of the sexual crimes of his father. Collin was quick tempered, aggressive, and antagonistic in his manner, but resorted to intimidation more than force to get what he wanted. One correctional officer said it this way, "Collin's bark is worse than his bite. Once ya know that, ya don't pay'em no mind." The officer's comment was validated in the first meeting between Collin and the researcher. When asked how about his youth, he replied to the researcher, "Screw you. Who the hell wants to know, you son-a-bitch." During the interview Collin revealed that he, too, was a sexual predator but not at the level of his father, for instance:

> "But she [the individual he raped] made me so horny, I went home and screwed my ol'e lady to death. I member…something though…screw'en my ol'e lady…I 'membered that little babe's eyes. They were mmm, pretties real pretties and gentle like."

Collin's comments were typical of the other family members. His descriptions characterized a preference for vaginal penetration but sodomy

---

49. The records showed that they had been married when he was 17 and she was 15. They had two children, one who lived with her and the other died at birth. The death of the infant was being investigated by state authorities. Mary Allen Quick's younger sister also lost a child at birth under similar circumstances.

was part of the process. Each family offender member, rarely used vulgar adjectives to describe victims. They were intense men who characterized emotional feelings for their victims.

Collin revealed that he had attacked four girls all of whom were unknown to him. He staked them, and intimated them into sex when an opportunity arose. Collin was easily frightened by females who strike him during his attacks resulting in his retreat. He was never apprehended for sexual assault. During classification processes, initially when he entered prison for the first and during reviews of his classification, he made it clear that the personnel case workers and staff were "ten light years behind me." That is, they were easy pray to his manipulations and only twice had be been caught in a lie while incarcerated which on one occasion lead to his physical beating by the COs. The way it was explained indicated that the COs would play games with the inmates by calling roll call at different hours, lock down and meals served off schedule, and they would watch inmates as they experienced difficulties with those changes. Then they would approach the inmate and verbally break the inmate to a point of violation such as cussing at the officers. Collin said that he usually was strong enough to resist taunting from the COs.

Collin revealed that had a sexual affair with his male high school teacher when he was in high school. Collin enjoyed the relationship "although I knew it was bad." Yet the teacher "would let me do anything I wanted." That is, Collin got to drive the teacher's car, spend his money, and bought his friends to the teacher's apartment. One time, Collin reported that he and the teacher went to a party thrown by the teacher's friends, after he graduated high school. They went together, but the teacher left Larry at the party. Larry was confronted by several of the party goers. "I was playing shy with them. Ya know. Saying I didn't know what they were talking about. I pretended to be stupid and pure. That's when they attacked me. They finished me off (brought him to an ejaculation) on the floor." He said that he enjoyed playing coy and enjoyed the attack "but that don't make me a fag," said Collin.

Tamara Evert

Tamara, Larry's twin sister, was recently released from an Illinois (adult) prison. She was a high school drop out but had excellent reading and writing skills. The researcher never had a conversation with Tamara. However, what was described by her brother, father, and jail keepers in Illinois where she was a prisoner until her release (no one knows her whereabouts), characterized an antagonistic personality. For instance, the jail keepers said that Tamara was always fighting with the other inmates and that once the fight ended, Tamara would question her custodians about the fight suggesting that she was an innocent bystander. One of the correctional officers said that if there was a "fight happening, sure enough Tamara caused it if even she wasn't there. She's a strange one. All the girls that come here go through a bucket of tears the first week. That one…hell, not one chilly moment." Tamara was a drug addict, highly sexual with everyone, and a convicted prostitute and thief. Steeling and sex were not pass times, they were obsessions. "She stole shit all the time and screwed any male who got it up," Larry said, "so much that folks wouldn't want her to come into their house. Hell, she was ripp'en toilet paper out'a school johns and she swiped the penny plate (for customers who needed a penny) from a Seven-eleven." There was a hint that Larry and Tamara had experimented with sex but the only confirmation was that Larry revealed that Tamara had a sexual encounter with another girl and he joined in. "But we's all stoned, ya know. I knew my sis was out there, but I ain't no weird moth'a sucker. I think she went down (oral sex) on me. I heard she gave the best head (oral sex) around. She worked it, ya know." Stephen thought she had a baby when she was 13 or 14, but Milton wouldn't confirm it or deny it. "That's her business," her dad said, "and if you want to know, ask her." She left the south and stopped in Springfield, Illinois in route to Hollywood. She wanted to be a "star," her brother offered. "But then she got hung up with some shit and went down on the wrong guy. Next thing I heard, she's doing time."

Jason King

Jason King, Henry George's son was 14 at the time of the two telephone interviews conducted which lasted a total of 45 minutes. Jason had a penchant for exposing himself to girls at the shopping mall and in school. His comments and the comments of the training school personnel suggested that Jason was a highly antagonistic individual. As one Division of Youth Services teacher put it, "Jason was high maintenance." Jason was compulsively conflictual in his dealing with others regardless who those others were. However, he was described as a loner by one of his custodians at the training school. His training school supervisor reported that Jason was always in trouble because of his "sexual attitude," but the supervisor would not describe what that attitude consisted of. One of the police officers who took Jason into custody reported that there had been a number of "peekers" (people looking in windows in the community) and masturbating while watching the occupants as evidenced by the crime scenes and reports of the witnesses. On one occasion, a "peeker" who was apprehended turned out to be Jason while masturbating as he watched a little girl play in her bedroom. The only reason the police apprehended him ("this time") was because he had not had a climax as quickly as he wanted it, Jason told them. "Ya know, I didn't get off," he confirmed during the interview. "What was more important, getting caught or relieving yourself," the researcher asked? "What was I supposed to do…it wasn't over," was his reply. Since Jason has been sent to training school, the officers said that there were no "peeker" calls in the community. "When we grabbed him, he didn't put up a fuss or nothing. He confessed on the spot."

Jason wrote a letter to the researcher explaining that he was not a sexual offender but some of the juveniles at the center thought he was. He had beaten two of them in a "fair fight" and asked his case worker to intervene with another boys. When the researcher visited Jason a second time, he said that when he fought one of the two boys in shower room, he forced that boy to perform oral sex on another boy. When the boy "was about to drop his load (an ejaculation), I kicked him in the butt as hard as I could and grabbed his penis, squeezing it down till he cried." Of interest: no one visited or called Jason (except the researcher) while he was at the juvenile center, his case worker reported.

Discussion

How can the criminal experiences of the King family be explained? They are chronically violent individuals who understand their feelings, their experiences, and the outcomes of their conduct. Their decision to commit criminally violent behavior is largely a conscious decision made in pursuit of their objectives which are centered in sexual intimacy regardless of the consequences for themselves or their victims. They continually survey their social environments for vulnerable prey. Once, they perceive an individual to be defenseless, they will attack when an opportunity exists. They can wait for an opportunity or if they perceive their intended prey to be approachable, they will attempt intimation and/or manipulation to lead this victim to helplessness. These skilled manipulators seek any weakness emanating from their prey. Once discovered, they turn the weakness against their prey and exploit them.

Therefore, most of the members of the King family are criminally violent predators who can be described as self-indulgent individuals pursuing objectives without regard for the welfare of others or themselves. Their conduct is largely a product from a continual process of self-interaction through individual interpretation of their social environment. They decide on a response that best brings them closer to their goal (for the moment), and do it–each limited by their physical capabilities, experiences, and expertise. Their conduct changes depending on how they see a situation or an interaction linked to their goals.

Why sexual assaults? It wasn't socially learned behavior as some admired scholars postulate since many of these family members had not lived together.[50] There may be another answer. This one lays with the issue that although it was 16 years ago when a researcher first called attention to sexual addiction, few sex addicts receive applicable treatment for their condition (Cares, 1983; Earle & Earle, 1995). All sexual offenders are not addicted, nor are all those individuals addicted—sex offenders. When sexual offenders assault others, victims are often troubled for life. For this reason, treatment programs for sex offenders should focus on preventing relapse at any cost (Laws, 1989). Nonetheless, given the high rate of recidivism among those offenders (often due to inappropriate techniques, mandatory treatment for those populations, under direction of governmental correctional systems is not entirely mandatory (Earle & Earle, 1995). When there are a few programs that do exist, clinicians shy away from the concept of sex addiction (Bureau of Justice Statistics (BJS), 1999; Earle & Earle, 1995). Clearly, something different is happening to most of the members of the King family and it might be prudent to argue that human behavior is a product of genetic inheritance and environmental circumstances. As such, therefore, some individuals like the King family possess a predisposition towards both physiological and psychological addictions which compel sexual attacks. That is, most of the King family members share a sexual addiction. They tend to relieve their internal tension, regardless of the consequences of their behavior and can not control the outcome of their conduct related to sexual assault without appropriate help. Since they have never received professional help for their addiction, it is unlikely that any of them could be successfully rehabilitated on their own.

---

50. For instance, Lee Ellis (1989) suggests that social learning theory of aggression is a psychological perspective that argues people learn how to behave by modeling themselves after others whom they have the opportunity to observe. However, this perspective is fatalistic suggesting that individuals who witness rape, for instance, have little resistance towards committing it. Also learning and doing are two different activities.

The sad truth is that abstractly there are many King family members in the United States, and they too have not been convicted of predatory acts for lack of an appropriate identification process nor have they been aided to help them bring their sexual appetite under control, assuming that is something they would prefer. Whether sexual offenders will be managed sensibly will depend on political action. Currently, politicians are reluctant to challenge the "get tough" attitudes of the American public and take a more effective approach to crime control for fear of being labeled "soft on crime."[51] A longitudinal study consisting of family members who are violent sexual offenders should be conducted. The problem is that to control crime, there are many hard decisions that require hard answers. Our choose must be to respond in a professional manner in keeping with the virtues of a democratic society who cherishes all of its populace and none at the expense of others.

---

51. For more detail on alternatives to punitive crime control see Beckett and Sasson (2000) and Glaser (1997). To learn about the social realities of violence versus idealized concepts see Brownstein (2000) and Toch and Adams (1994).

APPENDIX 1: STEPHEN'S GENOGRAM

Name	Age	Marital	General Reaction	Compulsive Behaviors	Disposition	State
Stephen's Parents	Unknown	Divorced	Unknown	(Father) Alcoholism (Mother) Extra Marital Affairs producing 2 additional siblings	Father Dead Mother Unknown	
Stephen King (Grandfather)	52	Lived with 2 Different Women	Laid Back	Sex	Incarcerated	South Carolina
Andrea Evert Mother of Milton	Unknown	Living with Another Man	Conflictual	Chronic Theft/ Alcoholism		
Lindsey Truman Mother of Henry George and Collin	Unknown	Dead	Unknown			
Milton Evert (Son)	34	Married	Laid Back	Alcoholism	Free	Florida
Henry George Truman (Son)	29	Twice Divorced	Laid Back	Alcoholism/ Gambling	Incarcerated	New York
Collin Truman (Son)	23	Divorced	Conflictual	Sex/Drugs/ Alcoholism	Incarcerated	South Carolina
Tamera Evert (Milton's daughter)	18	Single	Conflictual	Sex/Drugs/ Chronic Theft	Released from Prison	Illinois
Jason King (Henry George's son)	15	Single	Highly Aggressive	Sexual Exposure/Assault	Juvy/Traini ng Center	Ohio
Larry Evert (Milton's Son)	18	Single	Highly Aggressive	Sex/Rape	Incarcerated	New York

References

Akers, R.L. (1997). *Criminological theories: Introduction and evaluation.* 2nd Edition. Los Angeles, CA: Roxbury Publishing.

American Psychiatric Association. (1994). *Diagnostic and statistical manual of mental disorders: DSM IV.* Washington DC: APA.

Athens, L.H. (19992). *The creation of dangerous violent criminals.* Chicago: University of Illinois Press.

Averill, J.R. (1993). Illusions of anger. In Richard B. Felson and James T. Tedeschi (Eds.) *Aggression and violence.* Washington DC: APA. (p.171-192).

Beckett, K., & Sasson, T. (2000). *The politics of injustice: Crime and punishment in America.* Thousand Oaks, CA: Pine Forge Press.

Brownmiller, S. (1975). *Against our wills: Men, women, and rape.* NY: Simon & Schuster.

Brownstein, H.H. (2000). *The social reality of violence and violent crime.* Boston: Allyn and Bacon.

Bureau of Justice Assistance. (1995). Understanding community policing: A framework for action: August, 1994. Washington DC: US Department of Justice, US Government Printing Office. NCJ 148457.

Bureau of Justice Statistics. (1998). *Sourcebook of criminal justice statistics of 1996.* Washington DC: US Department of Justice, US Government Printing Office. [On-line] Available: http://www.ojp.usdoj.gov/bjs/sandlle.htm

Bureau of Justice Statistics. (1999). Criminal victimization 1997: Changes 1996-97. Washington DC: US Department of Justice, US Government Printing Office. [On-line] Available: http://www.ojp.usdoj.gov/bjs/pub/press/cv97.pr

Campbell, C. (1976, February). Portrait of a mass killer. *Psychology Today, 9*, 100-119.

Canter, D. (1994). *Criminal shadows.* Great Britain: Harper Collins.

Cares, P. (1983). *Out of the shadows: Understanding sexual addiction.* Minneaplis: CompCare.

Carter, D.L. (1991). Theoretical dimensions in the abuse of authority by police officers. In Thomas Barker and David L. Carter (Eds.) *Police Deviance*, 2nd edition, pp. 197-217. Cincinnati: Anderson Publishing.

Carter, D.L., & Radalet, L.A. (1999). The police and the community, 6th edition. NJ: Prentice Hall.

Clark, J.G., Jackson, M.S., & Schaefer, P.M. (1997). Training SWAT terms: Implications for improving tactical units. Unpublished manuscript, North Carolina Justice Academy. NC Printing Office.

Cohen, D.A. (1997). Notes on the clinical assessment of dangerousness in offender populations. [On-line] Available: http://www.priory.com/psych/assessin.htm

Collins, R. (1979). *The credential society.* Orlando, FL: Academic Press.

Crime Free America. (1999). Crime Forum. [On-Line]. Available: http://crime-free.org/index.html

Denno, D.W. (1990). *Biology and violence.* NY: Cambridge University Press.

Douglas, J., & Olshaker, M. (1995). *Mindhunter.* NY: Pocket Star Books.

Durkheim, E. (1933, 1984). *Durkheim: The division of labor in society.* NY: Free. Translation by Lewis A. Coser.

Earle, R.H., & Earle, M.R. (1995). *Sex addiction: Case studies and management.* NY: Brunner/Mazel.

Ellis, L. (1989). Theories of rape. NY: Hemisphere.

Glaser, D. (1997). *Profitable penalties: How to cut both crime rates and costs.* Thousand Oaks, CA: Sage Publications.

Goodman, A. (1998). *Sexual addiction: An integrated approach.* Connecticut: International Universities Press, Inc.

Gordon, M.T., & Riger, S. (1989). *The female fear: The social cost of rape.* NY: Free.

Gottfredson, M.R., & Hirschi, T. (1990). *A general theory of crime.* Stanford, CA: Stanford University Press.

Grant, B., & Curry, D. (1993). Women murderers and victims of abuse in southern state. *American Journal of Criminal Justice, 17*(2), 73-83.

Grasser, B., & Strauss, A. (1967). *The discovery of the grounded theory: Strategies for qualitative research.* Chicago: Aldine.

Green, A. H. (1999). Female sex offenders. In John A. Shaw (ED.) *Sexual aggression*, (p.195-210). Washington DC: APA.

Greenfiled, L.A. (1997). *Sex offenses and offenders.* Washington DC: U.S. Department of Justice, Bureau of Justice Statistics. NCJ 163392.

Greenwood, P.W., & Petersilia, J. (1975). *The criminal investigation process—Volume I: Summary and policy implications.* Santa Monica, CA: Rand Corporation.

Groth, N.A. (1980). *Men who rape.* NY: Plenum Press.

Hare, R.D. (1996). *Psychopathy and Antisocial Personality Disorder: A case of diagnostic confusion.* Psychiatric Times, 12(2). (On-line) Available: http://www.hare.org/articles/index.html

Hazelwood, R.R., & Douglas, J.E. (1980, April). *The lust murderer.* FBI Law Enforcement Bulletin. Washington DC: US Department of Justice.

Hickey, E.W. (1997). *Serial murderers and their victims.* Belmont, CA: Wadsworth.

Holmes, R.M., & Holmes, S.T. (1996). *Profiling violent crimes: An investigative tool.* Thousand Oaks, CA: Sage Publications.

Jenkins, P. (1994). *Using murder: The social construction of serial homicide.* NY: Aldine

Kruttschnitt, C., Ward, D. & Sheble, M.A. (1987). Abuse-resistant youth: Some factors that may inhibit violent criminal behavior. *Social Forces, 66*(2), 501-519.

Laws, D.R. (1989*). Relapse prevention with sex offenders.* NY: Guilford.

Lyman, S.M., & Scott, M.B. (1989). *Sociology of the absurd.* Dix Hills, NY: GHP.

Marongu, P., & Newman, G. (1987). *Vengeance: The fight against injustice.* Totowa, NJ: Rowman & Littlefield Publisher.

MacKinnon, C. (1987). *Feminism unmodified.* NY: Wiley.

McConaghy, N. (1993). *Sexual behavior: Problems and management.* NY: Plenum Press.

Michalowski, R.J. (1985). *Order, law, and crime.* NY: McGraw Hill.

Miethe, T.D., & McCorkle, R. (1998). *Crime profiles: The anatomy of dangerous persons, places, and situations.* Los Angeles, CA: Roxbury Publishing.

Monhan, J. (1984). The prediction of violent behavior: Toward a second generation of theory and policy. *American Journal of Psychiatry*, 141, 10-15.

Pallone, N.J., & Hennessy, J.J. (1992). *Criminal behavior: A process psychology analysis.* New Brunswick, NJ: Transaction Publishers.

Raine, A., Buchsbaum, M.S., Stanley, J., Lottenberg, S., Abel, L., & Stoddard, J. (1994). Research reviews and information on biological causes of criminal, violent, and psychopathic behavior. *Biological Psychiatry, 36.* [On-line]. Available: http://www.crime-times.org/95a/w95ap1.htm

Samenow, S. (1984). *Inside the criminal mind.* NY: Random.

Schmalleger, F. (1999). *Criminology today.* Upper Saddle River, NJ: Prentice Hall.

Scully, D. (1990). *Understanding sexual violence.* NY: Putnum.

Spaulding, D. (1997, March). Tactical entry. *Police*, 29-32.

Steadman, H.J., & Cocozza, J.J. (1980). The prediction of dangerousness-Baxtrom: A case study. In: G. Cooke (Ed.) *The role of the forensic psychologist.* Springfield, Il.: Thomas. Pp. 204-215.

Stevens, D.J. (2000a). *Case Studies in Community Policing.* Upper Saddle River, NJ: Prentice Hall.

Stevens, D.J. (2000b). Civil liabilities and arrest decisions. In Dennis J. Stevens and Mark Dantzker (EDS.) *Policing and Community Partnerships.* Upper Saddle Rive, NJ: Prentice Hall.

Stevens, D.J. (1998a). *Inside the mind of the serial rapist.* Bethesda, MD: Austin & Winfield Publishers.

Stevens, D.J. (1998b). Interviews with women convicted of murder: Battered women syndrome revisited. *International Review of Victimology, 6*(2).

Stevens, D.J. (1998c). Narcotic officers: A study of inexperience, virtue, and corruption. *The Law Enforcement Journal, 5(3),* Summer/Fall, pp. 58-69.

Stevens, D.J. (1998d) The impact of time-served and regime on prisoners' anticipation of crime: Female Prisonisation Effects. *The Howard Journal of Criminal Justice*, 37(2), 188-205.

Stevens, D.J. (1998e). Incarcerated women, crime, and drug addiction. *The Criminologist, 22*(1), 3-14.

Stevens, D.J. (1997a). Violence begets violence. *Corrections Compendium: The National Journal for Corrections. American Correctional Association, 22*(12), 1-2.

Stevens, D.J. (1997b). Influences of early childhood experiences on subsequent criminally violent behavior. *Studies on Crime and Crime Prevention, 6*(1), 35-51.

Stevens, D.J. (1997c) Prison Regime and Drugs. *The Howard Journal of Criminal Justice,* 36(1), 14-27.

Stevens, D.J. (1994) The depth of imprisonment and prisonisation: Levels of security and prisoners' anticipation of future violence. *The Howard Journal of Criminal Justice 33*(2), 137-157.

Thornhill, R., & Palmer, C. (2000). *A natural history of rape: Biological bases of sexual coercion.* Cambridge, MA: MIT Press.

Toch, H. & Adams, K. (1994). *The disturbed violent offender.* Washington DC: APA.

U.S. Department of Justice. (1999a). Sixty percent of convictred sex offenders are on parole or probation. NCJ 163392. (On Line) Available: http://www.ojp.usdoj.gov/bjs/pub/press/soo.pr

U.S. Department of Justice. (1999b). Rape and sexual assault. (On-Line) Available: http://www.ojp.usdoj.gov/ovc/ncvrw/1998/html/rape.htm

Weeks, J.R., & Morison, S. (1993). Offender typologies: Identifying treatment relevant characteristics. *Forum.* [On-line]. Available: http://www.csc-scc.gc.ca/crd/forum/e05/e051e.htm

CHAPTER 12

Predatory Pedophiles: A Case Study

Introduction

This study examines men who engage in habitual sexual conduct with children. They are referred to as pedophiles. Pedophilia is defined as intense and persistent sexual interest in prepubescent children (American Psychiatric Association, 1994, p.528). Some pedophiles seek same gender victims (homosexual pedophiles), others seek opposite gender victims (heterosexual pedophiles), and some don't care about gender.[52] The most common child molester sexually assaults his own children or those of someone he knows (Leberg, 1997). This type of offender is more concerned with committing a sexual assault with a child than concerning himself with the gender of his victims. As the assaults take place within a social network of well meaning and well intentioned adults, the molester's manipulations and criminality are never suspected.

---

52. For more detail see Proulx, Granger, Ouimet, Guay, McKibben, St-Yves, Bigras, Perreault, Brien, and Pellerin (1999) whose sample consisted of 197 sexual offenders. Seventy-one percent of their sample sexually assaulted children under the age of 17 with the vast majority of those victims under the age of 12. There were almost as many step fathers sexually attaching their children as there were offenders attaching acquaintances. Homosexual pedophiles attached their own children as offend as others attached strangers and acquaintances, however, heterosexual pedophiles attached family members more often than strangers (Proulx et al, 1999)

One concern of this work is that as predators move into new neighborhoods, despite all of the official precautions of the criminal justice community to rehabilitate them and to warn the public about their presence through Megan's Law type vehicles, these child molesters continue to sexually attack children. Many individuals hold an assumption that law enforcement controls the streets when in fact, the experiences of many officers suggest that this assumption is unlikely to be supported (Stevens, 2001b, 1999a, 1999b). One goal of this work, therefore, is to explain the primary social and psychological characteristics of a typical pedophile to better understand how many of them are undetected and those who are apprehended and convicted, tend to gain support from others even to the extent of others defending their innocence.[53] According to DSM-IV, "the onset of pedophilia usually begins in adolescence," and its course is "usually chronic." However, one compelling argument suggests that the personality of a violent offender is a product of biological inheritance, culture, environment, and common and unique experiences (Holmes & Holmes, 1990).

Child molesters arrive at deviancy via multiple pathways and engage in many different sexual and nonsexual "acting out" behaviors with children ("Child sexual…," 2000). No single "molester profile" exists, some writers speculate. That is, child molesters are highly dissimilar in terms of personal characteristics, life experiences, and criminal histories. Yet, their decisions to commit specific sexual crimes are similar even though they make different decisions about their lifestyles.

---

53. The researcher acknowledges that there is great resistance in accepting the evidence in this work since the scientific literature tends to rely on established perspectives more often even when those perspectives might be inadequate especially among sexual offenders (McConaghy, 1997).

Statistics

Government status showed that on a given day in 1994 there were approximately 234,000 offenders convicted of rape or sexual assault under the care, custody, or control of correctional agencies (Bureau of Justice Statistics (BJS), 2000). Approximately, 60% of these sex offenders are under conditional community supervision. The median age of the victims of imprisoned sexual assaulters was less than 13 years old. The median age of rape victims was about 22 years. An estimated 24% of those serving time for rape and 19% of those serving time for sexual assault had been on probation or parole at the time of the offense for which they were placed in a state prison in 1991.

Offenders who had victimized a child were on average 5 years older than the violent offenders who had committed their crimes against adults (BJS, 2000). Nearly 25% of child victimizers were age 40 or older, but about 10% of the inmates with adult victims fell in that age range.

Legislation

Recent legislation in several states providing correctional supervision including rehabilitative treatment has stirred legal, clinical, and public policy controversies (Grossman, Martis & Fichtner, 1999). Some perspectives show that few treatments work. Accordingly, some state correctional systems such as the Illinois Department of Corrections are holding sexual offenders after those offenders maxed their prison time until DOC clinicians can confirm those offenders are no longer a threat to society (Chicago Tribune, 1999). Outcome research suggests a reduction in recidivism of 30% over seven years and institutionally based treatment is associated with poorer outcome than outpatient treatment (Grossman, Martis & Fichtner, 1999). While other writers proclaim that they have reliable evidence that sexual offenders who attend and cooperate with treatment while incarcerated are less likely to reoffend than those who reject intervention (Hanson & Bussiere, 1998). However, child molesters have been known to reoffend as late as 20 years following release from prison programs ("Child sexual," 2000; Forum of Correctional Research, 1993). Those who do reoffend, those researchers found, had committed more sexual offenses, had more deviant sexual interests—such as sex with boys or victimization of strangers, and did not complete their rehabilitative treatment programs.

Grubin and Kennedy (1991) argue that sexual offenders are an extremely heterogeneous population that has not on the whole been subdivided into clinically meaningful groups. A sexual offense, whether pedophilia, rape, or indecent exposure are legal terms for describing this complex behavior. It tells little about the individual who carries out those complex acts, and which methods of intent are followed. Yet, we tend to think in terms of child molesters as members of a group and base our understanding of their behavior on that one aspect of their conduct: victim selection.

Control Strategies

Elaborate strategies across the country have been established to control sexual offenders. For instance, in Tampa a working partnership was created between several criminal justice agencies and community groups to keep trace of released and known sexual predators (McNamara, 2000). One method called for an intensive program of monitoring identified and released predators which includes the dissemination of all relevant material to parole and probation officers as well as neighborhood watch groups. With federal funds designated for a community policing initiative, police officials established a Firehouse Unit to conduct personal contact checks several times on a monthly basis with released predators. Here's how it works: an administrative day shift officer is the program coordinator when a sexual predator moves into the city limits, the administrative officer obtains information on every daycare center/nursery school and public/private school with a 1.5 mile radius of the subject's residence. Copies of the predator's photos are provided. Each firehouse officer will make monthly contacts with released predators in their assigned areas. All information is recorded and available to concerned individuals. "This information will contain a myriad of intelligence that can be utilized in future investigations if necessary" (McNamara, 2000, p. 61). To ensure accurate data are maintained, the administrative officer acts as the liaison between the Tampa PD, the Hillsborough County Sheriff, and the Florida Department of Corrections. Other agencies created an "omnipresent atmosphere" and a database in which pertinent information relates to sexual offenders (McNamara, 2000). And what good has come for Tampa efforts? One way to look at these programs might be to review some dramatic offender self-reported data on victimization rates. For example, from research in which investigators recruited 561 individuals who were not under department of correctional supervision, 291,737 "paraphilic acts" committed against 195,407 victims under the age of 18 were reported (Abel, Becker, Mittelman, Cummingham-Rathner, Rouleau, & Murphy, 1987). Not overpathologizing children's sexual behaviors has become even more critical in the 1990s when many states were registering youths as sexual predators regardless of age. For instance, Colorado maintains a database in the Central Registry in which all persons who have a sustained petition of sexual abuse against them are registered as sexual predators. Person's name remains in the registry for life. Children as young as six have been listed in the Central Registry (Johnson, 1999). At issue is the idea that there are distinctive differences between the behavioral characteristics of sexual victims and sexual predators among children. One conclusion drawn from that research is that few offenders commit a high percent of the sexual assaults against children.

Personality Tests

Furthermore, many researchers are under an impression that convicted sexual offenders will sit down and take a personality test such as a MMPI or a (MCMI) (Gingrich & Campbell, 1995; Weekes & Morison, 1993).[54] From the results of those tests, assumptions are made about these individuals and about treatment. What is forgotten is that they are criminals–individuals who break laws to get what they want and breaking a testing norm–fabricating the truth is not beyond their grasp. Of course, that's only part of the naive assumptions promoted by unsuspecting experts. The other part is that of an identification of a sexual predator. Chances are that most sexual predators including pedophiles are rarely apprehended and when they are, it is unlikely that they are identified as a sexual predator, earlier studies have found (Stevens, 2001a, 2000a, 1998a). There are several reasons for this including plea bargaining practices since 90% of most cases are plead out (BJS, 2000). Other factors relate to the institutional blindness of the criminal justice community and the sophistication levels of predators. First, a little information about the pedophiles in this case study will be revealed.

Sample

To operationalize the realities of pedophiles, three convicted predators will help guide our understanding of these offenders. The cases of all three participants were high profile events in the region of the country where

---

54. MCMI or Millon Clinical Multiaxial Inventory consists of a 175-item, paper-and-pencil self-report questionnaire designed to measure psychopathology. The MCMI produces a personality profile based on 20 personality dimensions. Also see Stevens (1999b) whereby Myers-Briggs Personality Tests failed to identify significant differences between convicts, cops, and college students.

these individuals were apprehended, tried, and eventually convicted. Newspaper, television, and magazines carried accounts of some of the incidents of their cases and continue to do so. Names, places, and events have been changed to protect the participants, none of whom knew they would appear on these pages. Two offenders, Larry Evert 20, a heterosexual pedophile, and Jason King 17, a homosexual pedophile, were participants in an earlier study (Stevens, 2001a, 2000a). The third offender, Sully Lexington 45, also primarily a homosexual pedophile, is a recent addition as a participant for the researcher. All three offenders are currently incarcerated sexual offenders in high custody level penitentiaries in different states. The relationship between the writer and the participants is that of a prison teacher and group leader to that of students and group participants. The writer has worked at many penitentiaries including Stateville and Joliet Correctional near Chicago, Attica in upstate New York, CCI in Columbia, SC, and Bay State in Massachusetts. While at one prison, the grandfather of two of the participants (Larry and Jason) was both an inmate student and a group participant. The third participant was a student of the writer for a five month period. The purpose of these three offenders is to help guide a discussion on the sexual characteristics among children and a discussion on the theoretical behavioral patterns of pedophiles. That is, while this paper is about pedophiles, the writer felt it helpful to utilize realistic models in order to better understand this complex and allusive criminal behavior.

Larry Evert

Larry Evert graduated from high school a year earlier than most youngsters by attending summer school and due to his performance level, which was higher than that of most high school students. He was incarcerated in a New York prison in the fall of 1999. Larry was highly aggressive during the interviews with the researcher, and a correctional officer described what characterized Larry as possessing a combative and antagonistic attitude. For instance, when an officer asked Larry to stop for a personal search, Larry swore at him and called him a racist (Larry is white). "Inmates don't conduct themselves that'a way, Mister," the officer told him. What was learned in those interviews can not be detailed due in part to space limitations and in part to the pending of other changes against Larry.[55]

The district attorney commented that Larry Evert is a sexual predator. He wanted Larry incarcerated for a maximum prison sentence. But, the DA apparently felt there was little evidence to convict Larry for the rape of a 10 year old child whom Larry had babysat while visiting his mother's brother in New York. Thus, a deal was struck whereby Larry plea-bargained to two Class E Felonies (sexual assault of a minor) and one Class A Felony (sodomy) for a four year prison sentence. The public defender argued for probation instead of prison. But, when the probation department of Larry's home state sent a report to the DA stating that Larry in their opinion was more than likely to reoffend, the public defender seemed to accept the lead of the DA. A comment by one of the arresting

---

55. For more detail see Stevens (2000a). Larry and Jason's grandfather, Stephen had three sons: Milton, Henry George, and Collin. Milton was a free man living in Jackson, Florida. His son is Larry who plea bargained two Class E Felonies (sexual assault of a minor) and one Class A Felony (sodomy) for a one year (no probation) prison sentence. Henry George was incarcerated in a New York prison and Collin was confined in South Carolina (different prisons) along with his father. Collin was a respondent along with Stephen in an earlier study conducted at the prison in South Carolina, although Collin was not a student of the researcher. Milton had a 18 year old daughter named Tamera recently released from an Illinois prison and 2 other children, but he did not know their whereabouts. Henry George's son, Jason was first adjudicated to a juvenile center in North Carolina but later tried as an adult and at 17 confined in a high custody adult prison, in protective custody. States and names have been changed to protect the victims and the participants

detectives was that if the police had not taken Larry into custody at that time that tomorrow Larry would probably commit a more serious crime. When Larry was apprehended there was considerable media attention about his case. He was detained in the county jail for three months before trial. He was on lock down most of the time. Once convicted, he was transferred several times within a few weeks to different prisons. Newspapers, television, and even the Associated Press covered Larry's apprehension and trial.

Jason King

Jason King was 14 the first time the researcher made contact with him to discuss his criminal activity. Jason had a tendency to expose himself at shopping malls, around the neighborhood, and at school. His comments and the comments of the training school personnel where Jason was confined suggested that he was a highly antagonistic individual. As one Division of Youth Services teacher put it, "Jason was high maintenance." Jason was compulsively conflictual in his dealing with others regardless of who they were. Jason has since been tried as an adult and remains incarcerated in a high custody penitentiary under protective custody due to his age and the seriousness of his offenses.

Sully Lexington

Sully Lexington had served 15 years of a 40 year sentence in a state penitentiary in a midwestern state for sexual offenses against nine children. They ranged in age from 3 to 6, and were enrolled in a day care center owned and operated by his mother. His sister worked there, too. Sully was a maintenance repair person at the facility that was also the home of his mother. From the testimony presented by one of the children, it was revealed that Sully dressed like a clown while abusing the boy. The child said that a robot at the school also bit him. Other testimony indicated that Sully used objects and photographed the children in the "magic room."

Both Sully's mother and sister were also convicted but in subsequent years released. Sully's arrest and court case were well covered by the media. Sully was enrolled in a business course instructed by the researcher at the prison.

Natural Sexuality

The development of sexuality during childhood is far too complex to conceptualize as a single entity.[56] However, it is expected that 40% to 85% of children will engage in at least some natural and expected sexual behaviors before age 13 years (Johnson, 1999). Natural and expected sexual exploration during childhood is an information-gathering process by which children explore each other's bodies, visually and tactually as well as explore gender roles and behaviors. Children involved in those explorations are of similar age, size, developmental status and participate on a voluntary basis. Although siblings engage in mutual sexual exploration, most sexual play is between children who have an ongoing mutually enjoyable play and or school friendship. It is the opportunity to be active agents of their own exploration and discovery. Their exploration is usually limited and their motivation is generally centered in curiosity. Sexual play is characterized through sexually reactive behavior that is essential to the natural and healthy development of sexuality in many children. All three of the participants had some of the listed above experiences, but presence of different components suggests their sexual play was not typical of the characteristics described. For example, Larry and Jason explored sexual play with other children both younger and older than them. Curiosity

---

56. There are seven lines of sexual development in children which are: the biological, change from sensual to erotic, behavioral, gender role and gender object-choice, cognitive understanding, sexual relationships, and sexual socialization (Johnson, 1999).

might have been a motive, but it wasn't a primary motive. For instance, Larry says what pushed him towards sexual activity was largely "because that's what I want. The thrill, man, strictly the thrill." Experience with similar offenders guides one interpretation of his thoughts (and other typical thoughts he shared): Larry held a mind-set about children and sex. That is, he was aware of what he wanted and of what he had to do to get it and little else mattered. Yet, he was never able to articulate why he wanted to sexually attack a child—that is, why the compulsion to continually experience the "thrill of it all?"

Problematic Sexuality

Neglect, abandonment, sexual, physical, and emotional abuse can all have a strong negative impact on a child's overall emotional and physical development including his or her sexual development (Johnson, 1999; Stevens, 1997a, 1994).[57] Although these factors do not have a permanent affect on sexual development of most children, their occurrence may require serious professional intervention. One myth that seems to linger about children's sexual behavior is a dichotomization of their behaviors into one group referred to as problematic sexuality. A misinformed consequence of this approach is that it is more likely that children with sexual behavior problems will be over-identified as young sex offenders

---

57. In fact, earlier research shows that that parents who continually quarrel steer a child to immediate gratification and loss of self control bridging that child towards future violence. In fact, incarcerated violent offenders reported that quarreling between their caretakers was more frightening an experience for a them in their early childhood experiences especially if lived in a female-rule enforcing household where parents were secretive and where these offenders were often injured. One implication was that neglect and abandonment through a lack of supervision enabled a child to learn social values that would lead them to subsequent criminally violent behavior (Stevens, 1997a, 1997b).

(Johnson, 1999). Victims do not necessarily become violators. Cathy Spatz-Widom (1989) argues that little evidence exists supporting the notion that victims become future sexual molesters. When children have had victim molestation experiences, often times their repressed feelings about those experiences might come out along different paths than that of a violator.

Nonetheless, these two groups within the problematic sexuality category were identified: children characterized as victims and children who engage in extensive mutual sexual behavior (Johnson, 1999). Some victims and some children (not victims) who do not feel a connection to their parents or other adults charged with their care might move toward peers for emotional safety. This lack of connection could be created in a number of ways. Larry's parents, although law abiding, never spent anytime with him while he, like Jason, needed the parental support to overcome his inner struggles. Sully lost his father when he was a young boy, and his mother served as his primary caretaker. Children can easily lose faith in adults when their caretakers are predominately self-centered, for example they rarely keep their promises. "I'll be home early and I'll help you with your homework." This idea is congruent with Gottfredson and Hirschi (1990) who state that people who lack self-control tend to be impulsive, insensitive, physical, risk takers, short sighted, and nonverbal. These parent/s tend to isolate a child from the daily family routines through a variety of methods, which include parental arguments. Consequently, the child can feel the affects of his or her parents' egocentric, hostile, and self-absorbed behavior.

Many comments made by Sully about his early childhood experiences suggested that he felt isolated and alone. His mother was rarely present as she busied herself with making a living, leaving Sully at age 10 and his younger sister to fend for themselves. It is likely that his conduct demonstrated at that time many of the characteristics of children who Stanton Samenow (1984) argues show signs of manipulation, aggression, and hold little regard or remorse for others. Samenow maintains that these characteristics among others can lead to an antisocial personality disorder, and are observable in some children at ages as early as five. It is also likely that Sully, much like Larry, had sexual encounters with his sister. For instance, Larry characterized his twin sister, Tamara was a drug addict, highly sexual with everyone, and a convicted prostitute and a thief. Steeling and sex were not pass times, they were obsessions, he said. "She stole shit all the time and screwed any male who got it up," Larry said, "so much that folks wouldn't want her to come into their house. Hell, she was ripp'en toilet paper out'a school johns and she swiped the penny plate from a Seven-eleven." There was a hint that Larry and Tamara had experimented with sex but the only confirmation was that Larry revealed that Tamara had a sexual encounter with another girl and he joined them. "But we's all stoned, ya know. I knew my sis was out there, but I ain't no weird moth'a sucker. I think she went down (oral sex) on me. I heard she gave the best head (oral sex) around." (Tamara was recently released from an Illinois (adult) prison).

Furthermore, if the early childhood experiences included sexual, physical, or emotional abuse, abandonment, or neglect, and they lived in environments that were suffused with intrusive sexuality, some of these children would seek other children in a sexual way to feel some form of comfort (Johnson, 1999). Sexuality is a vehicle that brings these children closer to their mission of a safe environment. Children try to develop a relationship of belongingness through sexuality with other children if they perceive that their family life was chaotic. There is little doubt that Larry, Jason, and Sully perceived their early childhood experiences as chaotic. Although, there were never in-depth conversations with Sully or Jason about those experiences. There were, however, indicators that could lead to that conclusion. For instance, Sully informed us (the researcher and the inmate-students) that his sister wanted him to play dress up and with dolls. But he refused. Sully revealed instead that he would stare out the window for hours wondering where his mother was. He said that his sister often pretended to be his mother during play and antagonized him to a point where he locked himself in the bathroom. He clarified with light laughter that he understood the difference between his sister and his mother.

It is likely that all three participants were predators seeking others through sexual exploitation in order to feel safe. The writer has no intention on blaming parent/s for crimes committed by their children. If those parent/s had time, knowledge, and training to deal effectively with high maintenance children such as Larry, Jason, and Sully, outcomes might have been altered. However, many children had led similar lifestyles and have not made similar decisions to exploit other children to their fulfill needs. Sigmund Freud (1856-1939) argued that we are goal driven, but the difference is that some of us make decisions in keeping with moral and social mandates and others make decisions in their personal best interests regardless of the consequences of their behavior (Samenow, 1984).

Larry, Jason, and Sully are more concerned with the benefits of their conduct as opposed to its consequences. This thought is consistent with that of other writers who argue that many violent offenders decide to commit violent crime centered in a single perspective: acquiring the benefits of crime (Gottfredson & Hirschi, 1990; Samenow, 1984). And Gottfredson and Hirschi (1990) add that crimes do not produce the results intended by those committing them because crimes are often opposed by their would-be victims. However, attacking children might offer different statistics revealing an impatience and suspect logic of pedophiles. For instance, one of the police officers who took Jason into custody reported that there had been a number of "peeker reports" (people looking in windows in the community). One peeker masturbated while watching occupants as evidenced by the crime scenes and reports of the witnesses. On one occasion, a "peeker" who was apprehended, turned out to be Jason masturbating while he watched a little girl play in her bedroom. The only reason the police apprehended him ("this time") was because he had not completed the sex act as quickly as he wanted to, Jason told them. "Ya know, I didn't get off," he confirmed during the interview. "What was more important, getting caught or relieving yourself," the researcher asked? "What was I supposed to do...it wasn't over," was his reply. Jason's impatience and poor lack of reasoning demonstrates some of the reasoning patterns of pedophiles.

Children require a model for a healthy parent-child relationship built on trust and caring. Parent/s who rarely keep promises add to a child's discomfort. Sully's mother for instance told him that she would help him with his homework, something he looked forward to, but she usually returned home late in the evening–then put Sully and his sister to bed as they usually fell asleep in front of the television set. This scenario is consistent with criminally violent offenders who tend to come from households where caretakers continually quarreled with each other (regardless of the caretakers relationship to each other; i.e. married, divorced, or just living together) placing a child in an unsupervised environment which could be seen as neglect (Stevens, 1997a). This neglect in and by itself especially for a high maintenance child can be a predictor of a criminally violent future regardless of the social environment of the child unless serious intervention is taken by caretakers (Samenow, 1984; Stevens, 1998b, 1997a).

Explanations of Criminal Conduct

Violence is generally viewed in relation to the situation that inspires it (Toch, 1992). Crimes of violence which include sexual offenses, can be viewed as interpersonal, and as a form of social conduct comparable to other forms of social conduct. Repeated violence is personally syntonic–a characteristic personal reaction, argues Han Toch (1992). The way Larry, Jason, and Sully react to their environments when not confined is similar to the way they react when confined. For instance, what was not revealed to the researcher in the original interviews for another study was that Jason had sexually attacked two boys at the juvenile training center where he was first confined. These boys originally harassed him when he arrived at the center. Jason asked his caseworker to talk to the boys on his behalf.

When the boys were instructed by a caseworker to "keep their place, and hands off," Jason took advantage of the opportunity by individually assaulting each boy and then forcibly sodomized them both.

Being a pedophile is a state of mind. One way to understand a pedophilia state of mind is to say that molesting children is practiced by some individuals with the same consistency that persuasion, or retreat, or self insulation, or humor, or defiance is employed by others. That is, sexual assaults are normal responses toward victims for some individuals and their response is linked to their personality which in turn is fueled by goal fulfillment. We are goal driven and oriented in our experiences, limited by our culture and both our mental and physical capacities. To bring evidence to this perspective that pedophilia is, from the perspective of the offender, a normal reaction to others centered in goals, Jason, for instance, wrote a letter to the researcher explaining that he was not a sexual offender but some of the boys at the juvenile center thought he was because of the sexual attacks he visited on the two boys mentioned above. There was nothing in his behavior, he implied, that was deviant or morally inappropriate. When the researcher visited Jason a second time, he revealed that he was involved in yet another sexual attack in the shower. He forced a boy to perform oral sex on another boy. When the boy "was about to drop his load (ejaculate), I kicked him in the butt as hard as I could and grabbed his penis, squeezing it down till he cried." Jason said that he had not provoked the fight, but evidence specks to an initial attack conducted by Jason. Furthermore, Jason explained that his sexual attacks at the training center and elsewhere were expected by his victims. His attacks were welcomed by them. "They enjoyed it," he claimed, and added he was only "doing what came natural."

Other writers advocate that criminals are not born with a propensity towards crimes of violence, but rather through trial and error, learn criminal activities (Bandura, 1973).[58] Certainly, an individual has to learn how

---

58. The social learning theory of aggression is a psychological perspective that says people learn how to behave by modeling themselves after others whom they

to commit a violent act since the act in itself is not a natural event but one that takes practice in order to learn the nuances of an attack. Children practice the ritual of violence and as they succeed, due in part to their goals, lack of supervision, and/or a lack of state intervention, the child can increase frequency and intensity of their criminal act. They learn ways of satisfying themselves and execute those decisions no matter the consequences of their conduct (Samenow, 1984, 1989; Cornish & Clarke, 1986). For instance, conduct is largely a product of thinking. "Everything we do is preceded, accompanied, and followed by thinking" (Samenow, 1984, pp. 6).

A question often asked is: were Larry, Jason, and Sully born as pedophiles? That can not be answered with a firm yes or no, but there appears to be a predisposition towards sexual attacks and/or violence that can be controlled or guarded to some extent during the formative years (up to age 7) of the child. It takes both, a caretaker and a child (children manipulate their environments too) to make a conscience effort to alter or control aggressive behavior from showing itself. The fact is that many children come from similar environments as Larry, Jason, and Sully and they too never received appropriate supervision; yet, they made decisions that kept them from sexually exploiting others for their own safety. The burden of guilt is on the offender.

Nonetheless, earlier research on sexual offenders, specifically predatory rapists, offers a compelling argument that criminal conduct is largely a continual process of self-interaction through an individual interpretation of one's social environment. This implication is somewhat consistent with earlier research arguing that "each of us decide on a response that best brings us closer to our goal (for the moment), and do it—limited by our

---

have the opportunity to observe. In this view, aggression is instrumental or a devise rather than the goal itself, reports Albert Bandura (1973). Therefore, some rapists, Bandura's supporters would say, can have a genuine appetite for sex, but are socially trained to use violence to show that they are serious about their goals.

physical capabilities, personal experiences, and level of expertise. Behavior changes depending on how we see or interpret a situation linked to our goals" (Stevens, 1998a, pp. 97). Therefore, criminal sexual conduct including pedophilia is largely a conscious decision made by a predator in pursuit of goals despite the certainty that those goals or what can be referred to as intentions are distorted.[59] If those interpretations are clouded by a compulsive addiction, then the reasoning processes of an individual could be blurred and distorted, and yet rationalized in order to neutralize responsibilities concerning their individual conduct. Could pedophilia become an addiction? Perhaps so, since evidence in an earlier study suggested that this argument serves as a plausible explanation among serial rapists (Stevens, 2001a, 2000a, 1998a).

Clearly, sexual offenders in general articulate a certain way of viewing the world and as such it can be considered an indicator of their cognitive structure (Benson, 1985; Durkin & Bryant, 1999; Pogrebin, Poole, & Martinez, 1992; Samenow, 1984). One striking characteristic of pedophiles is their ability to minimize or rationalize their activities (Mayer, 1985). Fact is, pedophiles have "an entire set of beliefs that they feel justify sex between a child and an adult" (Abel, Becker, & Cunningham-Rathner, 1984, p.89). For example, many of Larry's descriptions can be characterized as sexual aggression towards females. He described a physical attack on a 14 year old girl who refused his sexual advances during a different episode of sexual activity other than the one conviction he already had received. Larry claims that he knows "what girls want and I know how to convince them they're right." Larry made little effort to hide his attitude about females and how they should serve males. "There's only one time a babe

---

59. Gary Heidnik who electrocuted one women while she stood in a pool of water by pushing an electrical cord against her and tortured and killed many others in the basement of his home might illustrate a specific example a psychotic predator (Schmalleger, 1999).

should open her mouth, and that's to......" "Babes? How old is a babe?" the researcher asked. "That's it man. Doing that (oral sex), they can be any age," was his response. "There's no evidence."

Their distorted belief systems of pedophiles manifest themselves in the explanatory statements they offer for their orientation and behavior (Durkin & Bryant, 1999). This finding, much like the finding that many sexual offenders were sexual victims when they were younger, should come as no surprise. Presenting positive aspects of their crimes or socially approved scenarios about their motivation for those crimes would both, justifies their conduct to others and serves to neutralize their penalties (Sykes & Matza, 1988). Pedophiles have good reason to want others to believe their lies since sexual offenders especially pedophiles are considered by most cultures including prison cultures to be among the most degenerate of all criminals (Bryant, 1982). While in prison, Sully, for instance, took a lover for protection who turned on Sully and offered him to the highest bidder. DOC transferred Sully to another prison when it became evident that Sully was targeted for continual attacks by other inmates. At his new prison, Sully again took a lover in trade for protection, and this time made sure that his protector asked his permission for everything.

Heterosexual pedophiles reminisce often and want to start their life over again while homosexual pedophiles tend to reminisce less often and rarely want to start over. For instance, Larry talks about home and is in the past with many of his comments while Jason and Sully rarely discuss the past but seem fixed on their future. For Sully (maybe because of his age), his concern is to be paroled this year and resume his position among his family members (married with three children). Sully despite the 15 years he has been incarcerated, does not wish to start his life over. Something the researcher found unusual among inmates.

Another key characteristic of a child molester is that he tends to demonstrate immaturity but the homosexual pedophile significantly demonstrates immaturity more often than the other pedophiles to a point where they prefer to act as if they were a child themselves. These offenders engaged in child to child interaction. However, heterosexual pedophiles prefer to maintain an adult role or status and behaved much like a mentor rather than a child themselves. The homosexual offenders were more often loners than the others, yet both groups of pedophiles enjoy children's activities. Homosexual offenders long for childhood and identified themselves as failing as adults. Lastly, pedophiles seem to demonstrate a more procriminal sentiment towards their victims (Wilson, 1999). That is, they characterize empathy for children—an emotional bond developed between the child molester and his victim. Neither Jason nor Larry, however, did not demonstrate this emotional bond while Sully was somewhat melancholy when we discussed parenting roles of business professionals in general (he could have been thinking of his own children, but he would fade out–become expressionless, glance to the floor, then start smiling moments later).

When released from prison, the molester usually returns to that same place he left and continues to interact with the same group of people. Sully talks about his family including his children and one could wonder about his relationship with them. Then, too, of those career violent offenders who can, they tend to select occupations such as medical doc-tors, child day-care operators, and police officers where the population they wish to exploit is abundant and can be manipulated or compromised into compliance (Gottfredson & Hirschi, 1990).

Realities of Pedophiles: Goals

There are two preeminent goals that convicted child molesters harbor above all others. First, sex offenders try to be where children are such as through volunteer work at abuse centers, fitness centers such as the YMCA, and occupations at police agencies, schools, and daycare centers. This thought is consistent with Eric Leberg (1999) a probation and parole officer in Washington who adds that what a convicted child molester wants most once released is that everyone accepts him back into society with no awareness, knowledge, or discussion about his criminal activities. When a person does have some idea of his sexual assault history, the offender hopes that that person will accept on blind faith his denial or distorted admission of guilt.

The second goal of an incarcerated pedophile is to avoid professional criminal counselors who can see through their smoke screens. One method pedophiles use to hide in prison is behind the role of a jail house lawyer (Leberg, 1999). Convicted felons have been through the system and sat through many trails. These are men who have spent years in prison with others of a similar fate. They learn about the law, the system, the (inexperienced) counselors and caseworkers, but they usually think they know a great deal more than they do. They press for every advantage they can muster when sparring verbally with legal authorities of any variety, whether police, probation officers, lawyers, or judges (Leberg, 1997).[60] They can manipulate correctional personnel. For instance, Larry Evert's manipulative skills were revealed when one of the correctional officers discovered he was a sexual offender (SO) and told other officers about him. One afternoon when the cellblock of young offenders was empty except for Larry, four officers entered it and confronted him. "Are you a SO?" they asked. "I asked how they came to that conclusion," Larry wrote (in a letter to the researcher). "They didn't answer but I could figure. So I turned the scales on them and produced a piece of paper saying I am enrolled in the ASAT program (Alcohol, Substance Abuse Treatment). If the CO who told you that I was a SO was right, then what's this paper

---

60. Many pedophiles sexually engage older children. For an indepth discussion on this perspective see Blanchard, Watson, Choy, Dickey, Kallessen, Juban, and Ferren (1999).

about?…DOCS is mandated," he continued to write, "to treat the nature of the prison charge before any subsequent element and something about they can be sued if they didn't. The believed it. How can you trust a CO, I asked. I knew that piece of paper would come in handy."

Pedophilia is a way of life in that pedophiles are constantly setting people up, even after apprehension, trial, and conviction. That is, manipulation is part of their character. Sully, for example, continues to claim his innocence to the other inmate-students, the instructor, and to anyone who will listen. Sometimes student-inmates let things slip in classrooms. For instance, Sully indicated to the class that some lawyers who were "itching to make themselves look like stars" were going to take his case, despite the fact that all of the legal appeals have been denied suggesting that the legal process was unbias and fair.

Sully suggested that in the past, others came forward who also wanted to "shine, but" he was holding out for "Ivy League lawyers." In the prisons, high profile cases tend to attract outsiders who are trying to make a name for themselves. Sully, Jason, and Larry cases are not exceptions to this type of legal manipulation. (However, this writer has no interest gaining their freedom!) In Sully's case, these Ivy Leaguers are trying to argue that many of the children who testified against him were interviewed by a nurse who is a strong proponent of the existence of ritual abuse. Her interviews where highly leading and suggestive, not settling for "no" answers. Because of the nurse's suspect interviewing technique, these lawyers are working towards his freedom.[61]

---

61. One editor of this paper wondered if any of these lawyers would invite Sully to their home to meet their family members especially their children should they win his release from prison.

What Has Been Learned

One of the problems with pedophiles is that they know too well how many times they tried to quit molesting in the past, making promise after promise to victims and themselves that this was the last time, only to strike again. They know they will fail and at some future date they may really need some allies on their side: a child who won't tell; a mother who needs financial help won't disclose to the authorities; a probation officer or a judge will go easy on him. They're always "working people." They would isolate their victims in "magic rooms" and within their own families, too by finding children who had been abused before by others, and then attacking those children. These children are unlikely to point the finger again at another pedophile especially if it were a high profile trial.

They would play on the weaknesses of a child including using shame, embarrassment, confusion, and guilt to keep the child isolated. Plan B might include punishment, bribery, and special treats. They would create barriers between the victim and sibling/s or friends because they know that victims often disclose sexual abuse not to their mothers but to someone else, frequently sisters, brothers, or close friends (Herman, 1981). Pedophiles sacrifice or manipulate all their victim's other relationships in the service of their sexual activity: poor early childhood experiences, poor martial relationships, unemployment, and so on (Herman, 1990).[62] A child can be lead to believe that his or her molestation is acceptable through a reach and react technique. That is, knowing that children are curious about sexuality that is used in the employ of exploitation. If the child resists, the offender reduces anxiety through candy, hugs, and compliments.

---

62. Sexual offenders do manipulate and intimidate their victims into helpless situations or circumstances. Although they would prefer a helpless victim in the first place since they can fulfill goals faster with less effort.

Advice, offered by Leberg (1997) is to never underestimate the degree of sophistication that pedophiles use to entice children and their caretakers. They know how to invade personal space, how to confuse a child-psychology, how to blame the victim, and how to turn the tables especially to capitalize on circumstances. The know how to make a child gain his or her goal of feeling mature and grown up. They know how to make a child confess guilt, and how to use prejudice, misconceptions, and expertise against caretakers, teachers, and counselors who understand them. They seek children without a father in their immediate relationships (Leberg, 1997).

Moreover, it has been assumed that most pedophiles are isolated individuals with little or no social contact with agemates making many of them socially underdeveloped or what some might call childlike in some of their conduct (Prendergast, 1991). However, pedophiles are misusing the internet in several ways: to traffic child pornography, to locate children, to molest, to engage in inappropriate sexual communication with children, and to communicate with other pedophiles (Durkin, 1997). Sully wasn't using the internet 15 years ago, but once those Ivy League lawyers do their job, no doubt Sully will learn how internet works work great ease.

References

Abel, G.G., Becker, J.V., Mittelman, M.S., Cunningham-Rathner, J., Rouleau, J.L., & Murphy, W.D. (1987). Self reported sex crimes of nonincarcerated paraphilics. *Journal of Interpersonal Violence.* [On-line], Available: http://www.ncjrs.org/txtfiles/163390.txt

Abel, G.G., Becker, J.V., & Cunningham-Rathner, J. (1984). Complications, consent, and cognitions in sex between children and adults. *Journal of Law and Psychiatry, 7:* 89-103.

American Psychiatric Association. (1994). Diagnostic and statistical manual of mental disorder, 4th edition. Washington DC: APA.

Barbaree, H.E., & Seto, M.C. (1997). Pedophilia: Assessment and treatment. In D.R. Laws and W. O'Donohue, (Eds.), Sexual Deviance: Theory, Assessment, and Treatment (pp. 175-193). NY: Guilford Press.

Benson, M.L. (1985). Denying the guilty mind: Accounting for involvement in white collar crime. *Criminology, 23:* 587-607.

Blanchard, R., & Dickey, R. (1998). Pubertal age in homosexual and heterosexual sexual offenders against children, pubescents, and adults. *Sexual Abuse: A Journal of Research and Treatment, 10*(4), 273-282.

Blanchard, R., Watson, M., Choy, A., Dickey, R., Kallessen, P., Juban, M., & Ferren, D. (1999). Pedophiles: Mental retardation, maternal age, and sexual orientation. Achives of Sexual Behavior, 28(2), 111-127.

Bryant, C.D. (1982). *Sexual deviancy and social proscription: The social context of carnal behavior.* NY: Human Sciences Press.

Bureau of Justice Statistics, (2000). [On-line], Available: http://www.ojp.usdoj.gov/bjs/crimoff.htm#sex

Durkin, K.F. (1997). Misuse of the internet by pedophiles: Implications for law enforcement and probation practice. *Federal Probation, 61*(4), 14-18.

Forum of Correctional Research. (1993). *When Are Sex Offenders at Risk for Reoffending? Results of Two Long-Term Follow-Up Studies.* [On-line], Available: http://www.csc-scc.gc.ca/text/pblct/forum/e052/e052ind.shtml

"Child sexual molestation: Research Issues." (2000). [On-line], Available: http://www.ncjrs.org/txtfiles/163390.txt

Durkin, K.F., & Bryant, C.D. (1999). Propagandizing pederasty: A thematic analysis of the on-line exculpatory accounts of unrepentant pedophiles. *Deviant Behavior, 20,* 103-127.

Gingrich, T.N., & Campbell, J.B. (1995). Personality characteristics of sexual offenders. *Sexual Addiction & Compulsivity, 2*(1), 54-61.

Grossman, L.S., Martis, B., & Fichtner, C.G. (1999). Are sex offenders treatable? A research overview. *Psychiatric Services, 50*(3), 349-361.

Grubin, D.H., & Kennedy, H.G. (1991). The classification of sexual offenders. *Criminal Behaviour and Mental Health, 1,* 123-129.

Hanson, R.K., & Bussiere, M.T. (1998). Study counters notion that sex offenders are inevitable recidivists. *Journal of Consulting and Clinical Psychology, 66*(2), 348-362.

Herman, J. (1990). *Sex offenders: A feminist perspective.* In W.I. Marshall, D.R. Laws, and H.E. Barbaree (Eds.), Handbook of sexual assault (pp. 177-193). NY: Plenum.

Herman, J. (1981). *Father-daughter incest.* Cambridge, MA: MIT Press.

Leberg, E. (1997). *Understanding child molesters: Taking charge.* Thousand Oaks, CA: Sage.

Johnson, T.C. (1999). Development of sexual behavior problems in childhood. In Jon A. Shaw (Ed.). *Sexual Aggression* (pp. 41-74). Washington DC: American Psychiatric Association.

Marshall, W.L., & Mazzucco, A. (1995). Self esteem and parental attachments in child molesters. *Journal of Research and Treatment, 7*: 279-285.

Mayer, A. (1985). *Sexual abuse: Causes, consequences and treatment of incestuous and pedophilic acts.* Holmes Beach, FL: Learning.

McConaghy, N. (1997). Science and the mismanagement of rapists and paedophiles. *Psychiatry, Psychology, and Law: An International*

Journal of the Australian and New Zealand Association of Psychiatry, Psychology and Law, 4(2), 109-114.

McNamara, G.M. (2000, April). Sexual predator identification notification. *Law and Order,* 48(4), 60-62.

Parson, C. (2000, May 7). Sex offenders find no way out. *Chicago Tribune.*

Pogrebin, M.R., Poole, E.D., & Martinez, A. (1992). Accounts of professional misdeeds: The sexual exploitation of clients by psychotherapists. *Deviant Behavior 13*: 229-252.

Pollock, N. L., Hashmall, J.M. (1991). The excuses of child molesters. *Behavioral Sciences and the Law 9:* 53-59.

Prendergast, W.E. (1991). *Treating sex offenders in correctional institutions and outpatient clinics: A guide to clinical practice.* NY: Haworth Press.

Proulx, J., Granger, L., Ouimet, M., Guay, J.P., McKibben, A., St-Yves, M., Bigras, J., Perreault, C., Brien, T., & Pellerin, B. (1999). A descriptive profile of incarcerated offenders. *Forum of Correctional Research.* [On-Line], Available:

http://www.csc-scc.gc.ca/text/pblct/forum/v11n1/v11n1a3e.pdf

Samenow, S. E. (1984). *Inside the mind of the criminal mind.* NY: Random House.

Shaw, J.A. (1999). *Sexual Aggression.* Washington DC: American Psychiatric Press.

Stevens, D.J. (2001a). A case study of three generations of incarcerated sexual offenders. In Dennis J. Stevens (Ed). Corrections Perspective. Madison, WI: Coursewise Publishers.

(2001b). *Case studies in community policing.* NY: Prentice Hall.

(2000a) Identifying criminal predators, sentences, and criminal classifications. *Journal of Police and Criminal Psychology.* In Press.

(1999a) Corruption among narcotic officers: A study of innocence and integrity. *Journal of Police and Criminal Psychology.* Fall, 14(2), 1-11.

(1999b) Stress and the American police officer. *Police Journal,* LXXII(3), 247-259.

(1999c) Research Note: Myers-Briggs Type Indicator—cops, convicts, and college students. *Police Journal,* LXXII(1). 59-64.

(1999d). Interviews with women convicted of murder: Battered women syndrome revisited. *International Review of Victimology,* 6(2).

(1998a). *Inside the mind of the serial rapist.* Bethesda, MD: Austin & Winfield Publishers.
http://www.amazon.com/exec/obidos/ASIN/1572921293/002-5756676-8984421

(1998b). Incarcerated women, crime, and drug addiction. *The Criminologist,* 22(1), 3-14.

(1997a). Influences of early childhood experiences on subsequent criminology violent behaviour. *Studies on Crime and Crime Prevention,* 6(1), 34-50.

(1997b). Prison Regime and Drugs. *The Howard Journal of Criminal Justice,* 36(1), 14-27.

(1995) American criminals and attitudes. *International Review of Modern
Sociology, 25*(2), 27-42.

(1994) The depth of imprisonment and prisonisation: Levels of security and prisoners' anticipation of future violence. *The Howard Journal of Criminal Justice 33*(2), 137-157.

Sykes, G.M., & Matza, D. (1988). Techniques of neutralization. In James M. Henslin (Ed.). In *Down to earth sociology: Introductory readings* (p. 225-231). NY: The Free Press.

Thornhill, R., & Palmer, C. (1999). *A natural history of rape: Biological bases of sexual coercion.* Cambridge, MA: MIT Press.

Weekes, J.R., & Morison, S.J. (1993). *Offender Typologies: Identifying Treatment-Relevant Personality Characteristics. Forum on Correctional Research.*   [On-line],   Available: http://www.csc-scc.gc.ca/text/pblct/forum/e05/e051e.shtml

Widom Spatz, C. (1989). Child abuse, neglect, and violent criminal behavior. *Criminology, 27,* 251-271.

Wilson, R. (1999). Emotional congruence in sexual offenders against children. *Sexual Abuse: A Journal of Research and Treatment, 11*(1), 33-47.

CHAPTER 13

Criminal Profiles

Introduction

An important part of my morning practices with a former employer was to have coffee in her office at the dawn of many workdays. Although Dorothy is a mentor and her opinions are generally valid, I was always amassed how she was able to expertly philosophize about some criminal matters I might have been working on with my law enforcement students at the justice academy and the criminals at prison. There are many individuals—individuals who should know such as investigators and academics and individuals who pretend to know such as movie stars and paper back writers—asserting their knowledge about criminal profiling when in fact, there is a preponderance of evidence implying otherwise. Some of that evidence relates to the unpredictable and out-of-control violent behavior in this country while other evidence relates to custodial personnel who have few clues as to the crimes committed by the offenders whom they supervise and whom they release. Part of this notion is often experienced with case workers, rehabilitation workers, and psychologists who discover that what works with the typical client, fails miserably with a criminal population. To help explain offender profiles, I developed a Criminal Offender Classification not from the academic textbooks or the popular books written by former investigators but from the experts—the predators themselves while teaching and counseling them in high custody penitentiaries.

The Sample

Sixty-one males and 28 females in two different high custody peniten-tiaries. The males admitted to 316 stranger rapes. A closer estimate of rapes committed by these individuals is estimated at 28 each or 1,708. However, records show that only 28% (17) of these individuals were con-victed of one count of sexual assault and none were convicted of sexual assault of a child although many of them had raped children of all ages. Only 5% (3) of these predators were charged with a more series single crime (homicide).[63] All of the females were convicted of murder in the first or second degree and all had life with and without parole. And, yes, inmates lie all the time, but measures were taken addressing validity.

On what bases is a prediction valid that an individual will commit predatory crimes? There have been many differences of opinion about answers to that question. Also, it is skeptically reported by behavioral experts including the FBI that psychopathic personalities are causal factors of criminally violent behavior. A criminal predator might possess some of the characteristics of a psychopath or be diagnosed as an individual with antisocial personality disorder (ASPD; psychopath) characteristics. That is, a psychopath and/or an ASPD personality can be similarly defined as a self centered person who has not been properly socialized into pro-social attitudes and values, who has developed no sense of right and wrong, who has no empathy with others, and who is incapable of feeling remorse or guilt from misconduct or harm to others.[64] Yet, there are

---

63. For more deatil see D.J. Stevens (1998). Inside the mind of the serial rapists.

64. See American Psychiatric Association. (1994). Diagnostic and statistical manual of mental disorders: DSM IV. Washington DC: APA, for a closer look at Antisocial Personality Disorder which includes in its diagnostic criteria (301.7, pp. 649): a pervasive pattern of disregard for and violation of the rights of others and failure to conform to social norms with respect to lawful behaviors as indi-cated by repeatedly performing acts that are grounds for arrest; deceitfulness, impulsivity, aggressiveness, irresponsibility, and a lack of remorse. Also see Narcissistic Personality Disorder which seems to add to a psychopathic definition.

significant distinctions between ASPD and psychopathy to mental health and criminal justice systems. The FBI described ASPD personalities as an individual who displays a sense of entitlement, unremorseful, apathetic to others, unconscionable, blameful of others, manipulative and conning, effectively cold, disparate understanding of behavior and socially acceptable behavior, disregardful of social obligations, nonconforming to social norms, and irresponsible. But killers are not simply persistently antisocial individuals who met DSM-IV criteria for ASPD, they are psychopaths-remorseless predators who use charm, intimidation and, if necessary, impulsive and cold-blooded violence to bring them closer to their goal. I suggest that both areas (ASPD and psychopathy) inadequately relate to criminally violent predators.

Criminal profiles, the personality of a criminal, is centered in an examination of official records. However, most cold-blooded murderers, the story goes, meet the criteria for ASPD, despite the fact that most individuals with ASPD are not psychopaths. An unfortunate consequence of the ambiguity inherent in DSM-IV is likely to be a court case in which one clinician says a defendant meets the DSM-IV definition of ASPD, another clinician says he does not, and both are right. It is a commonly held perspective that since criminally violent sociopaths and/or psychopaths have been apprehended, convicted, and incarcerated that studies about these individuals are valid. Clearly, ASPD characteristics are very common in confined populations, and those with the disorder are heterogeneous with respect to personality, attitudes and motivations for engaging in criminal behavior—so, is it reasonable to assume that offenders have learned many of those characteristics through their exchanges with the criminal justice system. From these studies, personality profiles have been developed to help in the apprehension of other predators. Is the tail waging the dog? It could be argued that criminal profiles have little to do with other criminal acts and more to do with those individuals who were identified, apprehended, and convicted.

Frankly, there are few, if any substitutes for solving cases than experienced, competent investigators often aided by the information obtained by reliable patrol officers. If profiles are largely a product of incarcerated offenders and are shaped from the experiences of investigators arising from solved cases, then there may be some issues that need an explanation: (1) How many prisoners are free since most offenders are eventually released from prison? (2) Since prisoners represent a small percentage of offenders, how many violent criminals are supervised in other correctional programs such as probation? (3) Since most prisoners are representative of offenders who are easy to apprehend and convict, where are the offenders who aren't easy to apprehend or convict?[65] (4) Since 91% of most cases are plea-bargained, who is really certain about the offenses committed by many individuals? (5) If most victims fail to report crimes committed against them, then how do we know that those confined are the worst of the lot?[66] (6) Since the confinement process in itself produces violent

---

65. In part, this is due to Clearance Rates: a traditional measure of investigative effectiveness that compares the number of crimes reported and/or discovered to the number of crimes solved through arrest or other means (such as the death of a suspect). Government statistics show that 37% of all crimes were reported to the police (44% of all crimes, 31% of rapes and sexual attacks, and 44% of simple and aggravated assaults. These estimates are congruent with FBI's UCR data (BJS, 1998). (On-Line). Available: http://www.ojp.usdoj.gov/bjs/

66. For example, predatory rape is under reported for a variety of reasons, says BJS (1998). For example, 25% of the females who didn't report rape might say that their rape was a personal matter while another 10% would say that they thought they lacked proof. Eleven percent reveal that they were afraid of reprisals from their attacker. Also, 2% of those unreported victims hadn't reported it because those victims felt the rape was an unimportant event. Other reasons might include shame and embarrassment. It might be safe to say that women fail to report being victimized due in part to their feelings that they would, again, be victimized by others. That is, once a woman is raped and tells: a spouse or an intimate-other, friends, parents, and/or the criminal justice community, she is treated differently. Her behavior can be translated into more guilt. Also, since women have been treated as inferior to males throughout most of their lives by their fathers, brothers, husbands, ministers, and other women (to name a few), she might consider her victimization as further proof of her inability to compete

responses, can it be responsible for developing ASPD characteristics among many of the prisoners?[67]

One more point, prison demographics suggest that most of the crime that Americans hear about is committed by amateurs—garden variety type offenders. Specifically, most prisoners are poor, undereducated, unemployed young men and generally individuals of color, then it's understandable how they became incarcerated and convicted in the first place.

Predators

A perspective about criminally violent predators is that they can be described as self-indulgent people pursuing objectives without regard for the welfare of others or themselves. They are chronically violent individuals who understand their feelings, their experiences, and the consequences of their criminal behavior. One practical way to understand behavior, can be that most behavior results largely from a continual process of self-interaction through individual interpretation of one's social environment. Each of us decide on a response that best brings us closer to our goal (for the moment), and do it—limited by our physical capabilities, personal experiences, and level of expertise. Behavior changes depending on how we see or interpret a

---

and to win against males. Lastly, some females especially young girls lack experience in telling parents. What all of the above means is that we may never know how many females or for that fact, how many males have been sexually attacked by strangers. But, a good guess is that the number of rape attacks is far greater than anyone expects or wants to entertain. For more information on this subject see D.J. Stevens (1998, 2001). *Inside the mind of the serial rapist.*

67. There is little in the literature supporting ASPD as being a product of incarceration experiences. But, some studies show that prison experiences produce anticipation of future violent crime, once released by nonviolent offenders (Stevens, 1998). [On-line] Available: http://198.103.98.138/crd/forum/e101/e101g.htm

situation linked to our goals. Therefore, criminally violent behavior is largely a conscious decision made by a predator in pursuit of goals.

The behavior of a predator can be characterized as an individual of any age, who continually surveys his or her social environment for individuals who appear to be vulnerable. Once, ascertaining vulnerability, predators attack no matter the circumstances of their prey. Often times, predators utilize intimation and/or manipulation to lead others to helplessness, yet predators must first perceive that an individual has the inclination towards vulnerability prior to intimating and/or manipulating an individual.[68]

Findings

After the data were pooled and examined, two distinctive patterns arose: 75% (67) of the respondents typically characterized life long violent resolutions visited upon victims whom they perceived as vulnerable. Therefore, I will call them predators. And, 25% (22) of the respondents consistently described characteristics of constant victimization by their subsequent victim where ultimately within the continual give-and-take of that inmate relationship, these participants utilized a lethal response as a final resolution to end their own vulnerability. Therefore, I will call these respondents nonpredators.

Once descriptive yet similar behavioral patterns emerged from predator and nonpredator data, a typology was developed to better understand those patterns of consistent behavior. Predator and nonpredator groups were collapsed into the following categories: 28% (25) typically described what I

---

68. Gary Heidnik who electrocuted one women while she stood in a pool of water by pushing an electrical cord against her and tortured and killed many others in the basement of his home might illustrate a specific example a psychotic predator.

will call hedonistic characteristics, 26% (23) commonly described control characteristics, and 19% (17) consistently described what righteous characteristics (see Table 1). Hedonistic, control, and righteous categories along with the visionary category (to follow) were comprised of all predators, and of the following, situational and revenge offenders were comprised of all nonpredators. Sixteen percent (14) of all the offenders routinely described situational characteristics, 9% (8) typically described revenge characteristics, and 3% (2) typically described visionary characteristics.

Table 1   Categories   N = 89

Categories	Males	Females	Total Number	Percents*
Hedonistic	20	5	25	28%
Control	19	4	23	26%
Righteous	12	5	17	19%
Situational	2	12	14	16%
Revenge	6	2	8	9%
Visionary	2	0	2	3%
Totals	61	28	89	100%

* Rounded

Hedonistic Offenders

Twenty-eight percent (25) of the participants described hedonistic characteristics when they spoke about their criminal activities. Hedonistic offenders talked primarily about the trill of their crimes, and how often they were bored if they were not involved in some form of criminal activity. They made little distinction between violent and nonviolent crime, yet typically seemed to prefer robbery, rape, and extortion (some enjoyed torture) although they committed every type of crime as often as an opportunity arose.[69] Their frequency of crimes of violence was reported as often as

69. Clearly, a crime of violence typically requires intent, opportunity, and a victim. One commonality described characteristic by all the predators in this study

once a month and crimes of nonviolence such as breaking and entering and black mail were reported as occurring at least every two weeks. However, perhaps since the hedonistic offenders were older and seemed more mature than the others in the sample, they selected their victims with a great deal of caution in comparison to the others. In any event, one typically shared primary concern was that of detection, not by the police, but rather by their victims prior to their attacks. Evidently, the hunt played an important role in hedonistic criminality. Every crime met with their approval, no one crime necessarily took preference over another crime, and the crimes selected were specifically related to the particulars of the hunt and eventual perceived submission of the victim.[70]

Hedonistic offenders preferred to shock their victims and received pleasure when those victims experienced surprise or pain. For instance, Mike explained, "Well, sir, one time I loaded some real shit into a refer (marijuana) and watched this guy climb the friggen walls as the shit kicked in and grabbed his insides. Sooo sweet, I could'a watched that all day, but then I got bored and left his sorry ass down by the lake." Their attention span was limited, as Mike suggests above, and although their voice was generally controlled and they used concrete words to describe ideas (as opposed to general concepts), they seemed to be physically touching everything around them most of the time. For instance, during

---

was that they admitted to possess the continual (from their youth) intent to commit a crime of violence. Many of them waited for an opportunity which translated to finding a victim whom they perceived as vulnerable. Yet, hedonistic offenders consistently described characteristics resembling manipulation, intimidation, and/or the use of lethal and nonlethal force in an attempt to produce vulnerability.

70. Caution here. This does not imply that hedonistic offenders were always (1) capable of conducting any crime; (2) that they completed every crime they decided to conduct, and (3) that once they did attack or approached a victim including a vulnerable victim that those victims submitted (many didn't). See BJS (1998) for specific attempted versus completed acts of violence.

the interview with hedonistic offenders, their hands (and eyes) were always in motion—on the chair, on the desk, on their pants, on their shoes—helping them talk. There was often a connection between violence and gratification, and they often eroticized experiences. For instance, two hedonistic offenders reported that when they had killed someone they experienced a sexual reaction. The overall theme of hedonistic offenders was: "if it feels good, do it."

Yet, unlike the hedonistic males who attacked men and women, the five hedonistic women repeated themselves often and enjoyed articulating about their attacks upon other women. For instance, Fran said, "The sick-ass bitch screamed to her kids to run when I picked up the tire iron. The guy stood there and stared probably cause he was pussy whipped and wanted to see me hurt that loud mouth hole' of his-the sick-ass bitch." Another salient issue that arose with the hedonistic offenders is that they often played the role of authoritative (police officer, school principal, military officer) type individuals when they sought victims.

They could play a role of any given occupational group (if it furthered their victimization) in a moments notice (or during the course of a conversation with an unsuspecting individual). Of greater interest, hedonistic offenders unlike the others played the role of another criminal. For instance, Don traveled to other states once reading about violent crimes committed there by other offenders. He would imitate the particulars of the crime committed with a different victim. For example, on a 60 Minute type television show he watched scenes about a predatory attack in Kansas; did some research on-line and in the newspapers. Went to Kansas, committed a similar violent crime leaving the crime scene as similar to the attack he researched, and returned home to his wife, children, and his professional job.

Control Offenders

Twenty-six percent (23) of the respondents reported descriptions of their criminal behavior that characterized what I call control offenders. Inferiority and insecurity seemed to be the primary motivators for this offender. That is, most of these offenders said things in their interviews suggesting that they continually felt that they were vastly inferior or below the expectations of their family, friends, and peers. More—they typically described what appeared to be a belief that no matter what they did, they couldn't be a good as others. Perhaps they felt helpless, too. For example, Wayne said, "I tried in school to get through…I couldn't do it. My ole' man says I'd never amount to anything…and my friggen brother said I ain't not'ing, no how….no matter what I did…so, I quit. But I shod'em all who's the man—the first time I kicked my ole' man's ass…" Violence worked for these offenders faster than other forms of reputation builders such as an education. Reputations could be made in the second it took to pull a trigger. The insecurity they typically described seemed to be related to what other people thought of them. As these offenders aged, younger individuals constantly challenged them. Yet, it was more than their individual reputations that were challenged. Everything about them seemed, from the perspective of the offender, challenged. "Shit, the way I parted my hair concerns for some folks. But, they sa'en not a word kno'en I'm pac'en (carrying a weapon)."

What their victims thought made a difference to control offenders as compared to hedonistic offenders who cared more about what their victims did. Although intent to commit a violent crime was typically described by predators in general, control offenders would more likely respond to a threat of force to them than the other offenders. "The friggen prick said he'd kick my ass, so I shot the mothar' friggen punch," Emmit said. This would not of been necessarily a similar outcome produced by other offenders.

These participants felt most comfortable were they committed the crimes of aggravated assault, torture, and armed robbery. Depending on where they lived prior to confinement helped determine their crimes. That is, if they were urban dwellers they often committed car-jacking among strangers and if they lived in a rural environment they tortured relatives and farm animals. These individuals indicated that they committed those violent acts weekly along with an equal number of nonviolent acts such as breaking and entering, theft, and drug trading. Then, too, control criminals committed felony crime (Part I offenses in commission of another crime, often a misdemeanor) more often than other offenders. They benefited by obtaining money, power, and control over others. Just being in-charge was an important benefit for them. The interviews with these offenders was difficult as generally they were rigid in the way they thought about things (this is the way it is done) and they talked about the issues they wanted to discuss regardless of the researchers' concern. In the interview, it was as if each control offender had something to prove. They were intense in showing that they were in control of themselves and every-thing around them. They tended to be loud and, above all were angry and conflictual. Often, for example, they would misquote the regulations and if someone challenged them, it was, "hay, you ready to friggen die cuz you read it (the 'No Smoking' sign) wrong?" Their criminal attacks were described as brutal, swift, and without notice. They were also younger than the hedonistic offenders and one thought was that maybe they there could be an evolution into that category especially if these offenders matured and learned to relax. There may be an evolution of criminality among predators.

Righteous Offenders

The descriptions of 19% (17) of the respondents characterized right-eous attacks on others. That is, they were the "morality police," explained Perry. These offenders said that their victims produced "the circumstances and the conditions," accordingly, they administered justice on behalf of the community, Robbey argued. That is, typically these offenders held views about every issue although those views seemed to be set to further their own agenda and the language used seemed to explain their behavior as noncriminal. This type of criminal may or may not display signs of his or her discontent to the outside world, but on the inside, this criminal has a need to rid the world of what s/he considers immoral or unworthy.

One problem with their rationalization was that it appeared that these offenders believed they were right! This thought may be congruent with writers who suggest that the same person who tells the lie, believes it. For instance, "Drug pushers ain't suppose to sell to kids, so I cut his balls off," Collin said. Later in the interview, he explained that he sold drugs to the kids after he beat up the drug pusher, and added that he was "selling quality drugs." Typically these offenders tend to justify their criminal activities. Their purpose is to minimize their responsibility or penalty relative to the crime.

Also, often emerging from the interviews with righteous offenders was a notion that their victims had stroke a "silent deal" with them, one serial rapist explained. That is, some predators (and defense lawyers) often blame victims for predatory attacks. For instance, Wild Bill, typical of the other righteous offenders, said that his victims had made a deal with him. He explained:

> She looks good, real nice. See, man, I wants this 'hole, so I let her help herself. She did'em and walks, laughing—telling (her) friends she made me. I catch her later on a back street and lay the 'hole down. I goes som'en like you owe. She don't act nothing like she's expecting it. I knew she'd be sweet. How'd I know tat' hole was twelve! But I had the right to that snatch. She gets exactly what she asks for, my big d——. Wild Bill

Typically, righteous offenders claimed that they were innocent bystanders! Their violent experiences seemed to occur every 3-4 months and aggravated assault, their crime of choice, seemed every so often to lead to the serious harm visited on their victims including rape and/or death. Nonviolent crimes occurred daily for this group of offenders, yet in most cases it was difficult to determine what the crimes were since they tended to rationalize their behavior as being appropriate and their manner of presenting this information seemed couched in honesty and justice. "I couldn't believe what that grown man was doing to those children. I took a big risk, and all…then smacked him behind the legs. We ran like hell," Karen revealed. What she failed to mention was that the he was a security officer for a department store where she and her children were apprehended for theft. These half truths suggest that major felons have a faulty thought process in comparison to noncriminals. However, typically, offenders like Karen believe what they are saying is both correct and in harmony with justice as evidenced her response as to why she smacked the man behind the legs; "If the cops can't handle violators like that, I will." The restored order where none existed!

Two other typical characteristics were salient among righteous offenders. First, their descriptions compartmentalized everything. That is, everything had a place and if something were out of place, they had to administer justice. "Children need a loving father. He wasn't. I did the town a favor and killed him. Ain't no one seen him since." Millie neglected to add (until far later in the interview) that he was drunk and unconscious at the time she took a kitchen knife to her live-in boy friend. The other characteristics about righteous offenders is that they acted quickly with their violence. It appears that largely that the violence they administered was spontaneous, but they had made a conscious decision prior to the behavior to do the crime. For instance, Millie revealed later in the interview that she had cleaned her kitchen knife waiting to use it on her boy friend. Once the opportunity presented itself, she killed him and tried to explain her actions as related to battered women's syndrome or what I call situational crime.

Situational

The descriptions from 16% (14—12 women) of the respondents represent situational crime and covers largely first-time offenders who were convicted of the crime of murder under controversial circumstances. That is, these offenders reacted to repeated attacks by their aggressors, but they had not defended themselves at the time of those attacks so the courts did not see that actions as self defense. Specifically, at the time they took the life of their aggressor, they were not in imminent danger as defined by US courts and therefore were not acting, according to the court's perspective, out of a need to defend themselves. Rather, the characteristics described by the respondents show that murder was their response towards an individual who interacted with them over time, fueled by abusive progressive interactions that produced a continuum of fear reinforcing their state of helplessness; as a last resort, the respondent attacked her abuser when he was most vulnerable. That is, delayed murder descriptions are characterized by victims who were abusive antagonists, and if they had abused others as they had the respondents, they would have been arrested and convicted long before they met with their death. These individuals largely had not engaged in any criminal activity prior to the crime that sent them to prison. It appeared that self-defense would have been a more appropriate verdict based on their accounts (and records). When they did respond to their violator, their actions were swift and lethal. For instance:

> When we were struggling to make ends meet, he just screamed at me. When he was promoted to manager, he smacked me when I wouldn't tell my every move during the day. Then he threw his dinner plate at me when I told him I wasn't to be his prisoner. After that I stayed home and made sure I was

there by the phone or else. After a year or two that didn't satisfy him. Lauren.

As the abuse accelerated the reuse of isolation contributes to a continuum of imminent danger producing further helplessness.

Revenge

The descriptions of 9% (8) of the participants described what characterized a perspective couched in the motivation to "get even" or revenge. As such, rage was described as one of the vehicles that helped these offenders fulfill their criminal acts of violence which usually meant an assault that ended in murder, rape, or arson (felony crime). Those violent acts usually occurred for most of the participants once or a couple of times. They described nonviolent crime encounters monthly. Largely, most of the respondents in this category described what appeared to be an out of control temper at the time of the interaction between themselves and their victims. For example, Morry said that he arrived home early and found his wife with another man having sex. One word led to another, and the next thing that happened was, according to Morry, an arrest for aggravated assault with the intent to commit murder of both his wife and her lover. "I blacked out. I don't know what happened. I saw green and yellow lights in my head. They turned to white lights and then darkness. I felt the light as if I had no weight at all." Morry had experienced interactions such as these several times in his life yet attacking his wife and her lover was the first time that he had been apprehended. The records showed that Morry was "like a wild man," the arresting police reports indicated. Typically, Morry like the others in this category used their temper often as a method of rationalizing their behavior. However, what Morry also revealed was that his wife had been cheating on him for several years but had never, to his knowledge, brought home her lovers. Morry was convict of aggravated assault although his wife died as a result of his attack. One important point was that Morry never came home early. My guess is that he knew his wife was entertaining and had decided to kill her years prior and was waiting for the right opportunity to do it. One reason that leads me to that thought is that Morry had taken care of his financial affairs a few months prior to his attack, yet he evidently convinced a jury that he had "lost it," as he put it.

"Vengeance is mine," reported Wolada. "I caught my business manager do'en the do (having sexual relations) with another women. He give' her my dope, too. I evened things up fast. Killed that friggen man on the spot. But don't know what happened. Everything was like in a light show. Couldn't see anything." Yet, it appears that losing control of one's temper is a matter of rationalizing an act. That is, Wolada like Morry utilized their rage to carry out what they had already decided to do, attack a wife or a boy friend and so on. The temper or rage was real, turning it loose—another matter. Anger or in this case rage, can serve to legitimize aggression. In a sense, rage is an emotion that people presumably cannot control and therefore they should not be held fully accountable for their actions.

Overall, most of the individuals who described ragefull events as those actions that lead them to violent crime described what appeared to be an individual allegedly out-of-control most of their lives (not out-of-touch with reality). Targets of rage are typically another person or a human institution, or the self. One interpretation of this thought is that rage and/or this out-of-control temper, per say, can be voluntary; that is, turned on and off by the individual who wishes to utilize it as a devise to commit violent acts and avoid responsibility. Acts of vengeance arise from an elementary sense of injustice, "a primitive feeling that one has been arbitrarily subjected to a tyrannical power against which one is powerless to act." In a sense, that is what both Morry and Wolada have suggested and it fits with how most of the revenge offenders described as sound justifications for their crimes. These revenge offenders present very compelling arguments about their criminal activities couched in rage that very often they found themselves not be apprehended (or charged) for most of the crimes that were produced as a result of their rage. Revenge offenders did not seek out prey, and their victims were rarely individuals beyond their own environment. Lastly, their victims were largely involved with these offenders and part of their everyday environment.

Visionary Offenders

Three percent (2) of the respondents described characteristics of visionary offenders. These offenders like hedonistic, control, and righteous offenders were predators. That is they sought vulnerable prey to victimize. One male offender and one female offender obeyed the voices and signs as offered by "gods" or "devils." Their crimes of choice was described as aggravated assault leading generally to homicide. Those violent crimes occurred a couple of times a year—every year and nonviolent crimes were rarely committed by these offenders, they reported. Their benefit to commit violent crimes includes the idea to fulfill divine directives. The most salient personality characteristic displayed by these offenders was that they tended to be out-of-touch with reality (unlike revenge offenders who said they were out-of-control). When these individuals committed violent acts, it's safe to suggest that they became out-of-control, too. When both elements are present, legally it could be argued that these two offenders may be insane (insanity is a legal term not a psychological term). Nonetheless, visionary offenders tend to commit slow violent acts that may take several weeks to fulfill. That is, they describe low periods of time during which the tortured an individual. In one case, a visionary offender tortured his victims for many months (without ever being apprehended for those crimes).

Conclusion

In summary, in order for the 21st century to be safe from terrorists, predators, warring nations, and uninformed crime control policymakers, the realities of crime control including policing and correctional supervision require an astute and unbiased evaluation. Perhaps, American policy makers will allow professionalism to flourish among those who accept the challenge to serve and protect before it is too late.

Table 2   Characteristics of Criminal Categories   N = 89

Category	Motivator	Preferred Crimes	Frequency of Violent Crimes	Frequency of Nonviolent	Benefits	Salient Behavior	Style
Hedonistic	Trill Fun	Robbery Rape Extortion	Once or Twice a Month	Every 2 Weeks	Shock	Limited Attention/ Touchers	Con Slow Violent
Control	Inferiority Insecurity	Aggravated Assault Torture Am Rob	Weekly	Weekly	Money/ Power/ Control	Immature Conflictual Angry Rigid	Brutal, Swift, WO/ Notice
Righteous	Justice For Community	Rape Murder Aggravated Assault	Every 3-4 Months	Daily	Restored Order	Compart-mentalized	Swift Violent
Situational	Victimized Self Defense	Murder Aggravated Assault	Once/A Couple Times	Never/ Infrequent	Self-Defense	Helpless-ness	Lethal
Revenge	Get Even Regain Loss of Face	Murder Rape Arson	Once/A Couple Times	Monthly	Regain Control	Rage	Swift Violent
Visionary	Obeys Voices	Aggravated Assault Murder	A Couple Times a Year	Infrequent	Fulfills Divine Wisdom	Out of Touch	Slow Violent

Made in the USA